Barack Obama

Barack Obama

Michael Burgan

Heinemann Library
Chicago, IL

www.heinemannraintree.com
Visit our website to find out
more information about
Heinemann-Raintree books.

To order:
☎ Phone 888-454-2279
🖥 Visit www.heinemannraintree.com
to browse our catalog and order online.

Edited by Adam Miller, Andrew Farrow, and Adrian Vigliano
Designed by Kimberly R. Miracle and Betsy Wernert
Picture research by Ruth Blair
Originated by Heinemann Library
Printed in the United States by Corporate Graphics

14 13 12 11 10
10 9 8 7 6 5 4 3 2

Library of Congress Cataloging-in-Publication Data

Burgan, Michael.
 Barack Obama / Michael Burgan. -- 1st ed.
  p. cm. -- (Front-page lives)
 Includes bibliographical references and index.
 ISBN 978-1-4329-3218-3 (hc)
 1. Obama, Barack--Juvenile literature. 2. Presidents--United
States--Biography--Juvenile literature. 3. Racially mixed
people--United States--Biography--Juvenile literature. I. Title.
 E908.B87 2010
 973.932092--dc22
 [B]
                    2009018176
032010
005708RP

Acknowledgments

The author and publishers are grateful to the following for
permission to reproduce copyright material: Corbis/Brian
Snyder/Reuters **p.85**; Corbis/Greg Marinovich/Sygma
p.55; Corbis/Hugues Lawson-Body **p.50**; Corbis/JASON
REED/Reuters **p.93**; Corbis/Joe Wrinn/Harvard University/
Handout **p.53**; Corbis/KEVIN LAMARQUE/Reuters **p.73**;
Corbis/Martin Zabala/Xinhua Press **p.83**; Corbis/Obama For
America/Handout /Reuters **p.13**; Corbis/Obama For America/
Handout/Reuters **p.24**; Corbis/Obama For America/Handout
/Reuters **p.27**; Corbis/Obama For America/Handout /Reuters
p.49; Corbis/Radu Sigheti/Reuters **p.79**; Getty Images/Dirck
Halstead **p.21**; Getty Images/PAUL J. RICHARDS/AFP **p.90**;
Getty Images/Rolls Press/Popperfoto **p.11**; Getty Images/Scott
Olson **p.75**; PA Photos/Darko Bandic/AP **p.31**; PA Photos/
Erica Gay/AP **p.69**; Rex Features **p.77**; Rex Features/Sipa Press
p.44, Rex Features/Sipa Press **p.65**; Shutterstock/© Mike Liu
p.36; Shutterstock background images and design features
throughout.

Cover photograph of Barack Obama reproduced with
permission of Corbis/Jason Reed/Reuters.

Every effort has been made to contact copyright holders of
any material reproduced in this book. Any omissions will
be rectified in subsequent printings if notice is given to the
publisher.

All the Internet addresses (URLs) given in this book were valid
at the time of going to press. However, due to the dynamic
nature of the Internet, some addresses may have changed, or
sites may have changed or ceased to exist since publication.
While the author and Publishers regret any inconvenience this
may cause readers, no responsibility for any such changes can
be accepted by either the author or the Publishers.

Table of Contents

Some words are shown in bold, **like this**. You can find out what they mean by looking in the glossary.

A Keynote Address

Barack Obama gazed out over the crowded Fleet Center in Boston, Massachusetts. The Democratic Party had gathered there to officially name John Kerry as its presidential candidate for 2004. Kerry and his staff had asked Obama to give the keynote address, one of the main speeches of the convention.

Some in the crowd held signs with Obama's name on it, but to many of the people there and watching on television, Obama was a mystery. Unlike most of the speakers at the convention, Obama had never held a major public office. Few people knew him well outside of his home state of Illinois.

Just a few minutes before walking onto the stage, with the crowd cheering and applauding, Obama had felt nervous. As he later wrote, he turned to his wife Michelle and "mentioned…that my stomach was feeling a little grumbly."[1] Michelle hugged him and said, "Just don't screw it up, buddy."[2]

Barack Obama did not screw it up.

OUT OF MANY, ONE

Obama used his life story to tell the story of America. The country had long offered promise to immigrants from around the world. They came for education or for jobs. Their children could grow up to have even better lives. Obama described how his life was proof of that promise. He told the crowd, "My father was a foreign student, born and raised

> *"There's not a liberal America and a conservative America; there's the United States of America. There's not a black America and white America and Latino America and Asian America; there's the United States of America."*
> —Barack Obama

in a small village in Kenya. He grew up herding goats, went to school in a tin-roof shack."[3] In Hawaii, while studying at the university there, Obama's father met his mother. She was a white girl born in Kansas. They married and had a son. Obama was named for his father, he explained, "an African name, Barack, or 'blessed,' believing that in a **tolerant** America, your name is no barrier to success."[4]

Obama took just 17 minutes to tell his story and describe his vision of the United States. His message was that Americans are one people. He cited one of the sayings found on U.S. currency: *E Pluribus Unum*— out of many, one. Obama said, "There's not a **liberal** America and a **conservative** America; there's the United States of America. There's not a black America and white America and Latino America and Asian America; there's the United States of America."[5]

A NEW POLITICAL STAR IS BORN

By the speech's end, some of the people in the Fleet Center were crying. They were struck by the power of Obama's words and the way he had delivered them. One expert on public speaking later called it one of the best convention speeches in history.[6] Cable News Network (CNN) reporter Wolf Blitzer said that the speech "electrified the crowd."[7] Off the stage, Obama turned to someone and said, "I guess it was a pretty good speech, huh?"[8]

> *"The speeches are the easy part.*
> *The tough part is actually getting*
> *something done. And we've still got a*
> *lot of work that has to get done."*
> —Barack Obama

The speech Barack Obama gave on July 27, 2004, in Boston was more than pretty good. It made him a rising star in the world of politics. In that moment, some people believed that Obama had the potential to one day be president.[9] But Obama was still just an Illinois state senator. First he had to win his own important race, to represent that state in the U.S. Senate. "The speeches are the easy part," he told the *Chicago Tribune*. "The tough part is actually getting something done. And we've still got a lot of work that has to get done."[10]

The work went well for Obama. That November, he easily won his election. Obama's fame continued to rise, as he kept speaking out on the need to unite all Americans. Then, in August 2008, the Democratic Party chose him as the first African American presidential candidate from a major party.

Obama knew the United States faced difficult times. The country had been at war with Iraq since 2003. Troops were also fighting in Afghanistan. The **economy** was entering a steep decline, and hundreds of thousands of people were losing jobs. Others were losing their homes. Obama promised to change the government's policies and restore hope.

But across the United States, some people still wondered if the country was ready to elect a black president.[11] The United States has a long, deep history of racism. Several million African Americans were once enslaved, and they faced many challenges gaining equality in the decades after slavery ended.

The question of whether or not Americans would elect an African American president was finally answered on November 4, 2008. That day, Barack Obama was chosen as the 44th president of the United States, and its first African American leader.

Soon after his victory was announced, Obama spoke to the nation. He knew the historic importance of the day's events. But Obama also knew the country had work to do to solve its many problems. He said, "The road ahead will be long. Our climb will be steep….but America—I have never been more hopeful than I am tonight that we will get there. I promise you—we as a people will get there."[12] Once again, Obama had offered hope to the nation. ❖

*"The road ahead will be long.
Our climb will be steep….but America—
I have never been more hopeful than
I am tonight that we will get there.
I promise you—we as a people will get there."*
—Barack Obama

HEADLINES FROM OBAMA'S CHILDHOOD

Here are some major news stories from the time.

Kennedy Murdered

November 22, 1963 – Dallas, TX

Riding in an open car, President John F. Kennedy was shot twice at 12:30 PM. His car rushed to Parkland Memorial Hospital, but doctors soon pronounced the president dead. Police later arrested Lee Harvey Oswald for the murder. Kennedy was just 43 years old when he took office. He appealed to many Americans with his youthful energy and his belief that "the torch has been passed to a new generation of Americans."[1] His charm and wit also made him popular with many voters, and the news of his death stunned the nation.[2] Later in the day, Vice President Lyndon B. Johnson was sworn in as the 36th president of the United States.

President Signs Voting Rights Act

August 6, 1965 – Washington, D.C.

President Lyndon B. Johnson signed the Voting Rights Act of 1965, which restricts the legal efforts of Southern states to deny African Americans the right to vote. The law targets literacy tests and other obstacles that have traditionally kept many blacks from voting. This law followed the passage of the 1964 Civil Rights Act. That law forbids **discrimination** on the basis of sex or race in public buildings and schools. Its aim is ending segregation, or the separation of people based on race or other traits.

Civil Rights Leader Killed

April 4, 1968 – Memphis, TN

Reverend Martin Luther King Jr., the leader of the civil rights movement in the United States, was shot and killed this evening at a local hotel. Starting in the 1950s, King used non-violent methods to bring attention to the inequalities blacks face. He led protest marches and organized civil rights groups. King was arrested several times and faced the threat of violence throughout his career. In 1963 in Washington D.C., King delivered his famous "I Have a Dream" speech. He hoped for a day when "my four little children will…live in a nation where they will not be judged by the color of their skin but by the content of their character."[3]

Black U.S. Athletes Protest Racism at Olympics in Mexico City

October 16, 1968

Tommie Smith (center) and John Carlos (right) protest from the medal podium, on behalf of oppressed American black people.

400,000 People Gather at Woodstock, NY, for Music Fest

August 15–18, 1969

The Beatles, One of the World's Most Popular Bands, Announce Breakup

April 10, 1970

Obama's Early Years

The islands of Hawaii sit some 2,100 miles (3,379 km) west of the mainland of the United States. With its warm tropical breezes Hawaii is a vacation wonderland to some people, a place to rest and relax on sunny beaches. For Barack Obama, Hawaii is his home state, and the place where he first explored his roots as an African American. Hawaii is where he learned to ask questions about politics and the world at large. It's where he saw that people from different backgrounds could live together peacefully.[1]

Hawaii had just become the 50th state in 1959 when Obama's mother and her family settled in Honolulu, the capital. Obama's mother was named Stanley, because her father, Stanley Dunham, had wanted a son. Starting college at the University of Hawaii, Stanley began to go by her middle name, Ann. While she went to school, her father sold furniture and her mother Madelyn worked in a bank.

In the fall of 1960, Ann met Barack Hussein Obama, who later became the father of Barack Obama II. The son of a farmer from Kenya, Obama had won a **scholarship** to study in the United States. While he was a student in Kenya's capital, Nairobi, officials there saw Obama's intelligence. They believed he could help Kenya create a better society. The country was close to winning its independence from the United

Ann Dunham with her son Barack Obama, in an undated family snapshot from the 1960s.

Kingdom and needed skilled government workers. The officials, along with some Americans, arranged for Obama to study in Hawaii.

TIME OF RACIAL TROUBLES

When Obama and Ann Dunham met, race relations were not good in many parts of the United States. In most of the South, states passed laws that made it hard for blacks to vote. Across the country, whites with racist views denied blacks the chance to attend the best schools or hold good jobs. Some states also had laws that kept blacks and whites from marrying each other. In general, few people, whites or blacks, approved of mixed-race dating and marriage.

A few years earlier, some blacks had begun actively challenging laws that limited their equality. They risked arrest to draw attention to the problem and protested in the streets. This effort was called the civil rights movement. Ann Dunham supported this fight for legal rights. She was also fascinated with foreign lands and people. She started dating Obama, who was known in Hawaii as Barry. In February 1961, they were married.

Ann's mother had doubts about her new son-in-law and his foreign background. But she knew he was extremely intelligent. Ann's father, Stanley Dunham, later said that Barry also had confidence. He "could handle just about any situation, and that made everybody like him."[2] Still, neither parent completely welcomed the marriage, although they did not try to stop it.

WELCOMING A NEW BABY

Six months after the wedding, on August 4, 1961, Ann had a baby boy. She and Barry named him Barack Hussein Obama II. Ann dropped out of college, but "Senior," as her husband was called, finished school. He graduated in June 1962 after earning straight A's. He wanted to continue his schooling, and he won a scholarship to Harvard, one of the best

Mission to the Moon

In 1961, President John F. Kennedy announced that the United States would try to land astronauts on the Moon within ten years. The astronauts young Barack Obama saw in Hawaii were just one part of that long effort. Several years later, on July 20, 1969, *Apollo 11* astronaut Neil A. Armstrong became the first human to walk on the surface of the Moon. Back on Earth, millions of people around the world watched the historic event on television. Armstrong and a second astronaut, Edwin E. "Buzz" Aldrin Jr., planted a U.S. flag and spent about two hours gathering samples of moon rocks. Five more *Apollo* missions landed on the Moon, the last one in 1972.

universities in the United States. The school, however, would only pay for Senior's education, and not the family's expenses. He decided to go to Harvard anyway, even though it meant leaving his family behind. He was determined to get the best education.

With her parents' help, Ann raised young Barack—who was also known as Barry—and began going back to school. Mr. Dunham took the young Barry for walks and brought him to the beach or park. One of his earliest memories, Obama later wrote, was "of sitting on my grandfather's shoulders as the astronauts from one of the [space] missions arrived at Hickam Air Force Base after a successful splashdown."[3]

While young Barry had adventures with his grandfather, his mother completed her work at the University of Hawaii. She also divorced Barack Obama Senior in 1964. He was focused on the career waiting for him in Kenya, not his family in Hawaii. Young Barry would only see his father one more time in his life, but he sometimes received letters from Senior. His mother often told young Barry about his father's intelligence and drive to succeed.

> *"Lolo also introduced
> his stepson to new foods:
> 'dog meat (tough),
> snake meat (tougher), and
> roasted grasshopper (crunchy).'"*
> —Barack Obama

MOVING TO INDONESIA

While studying at the university, Ann met another foreign student. Lolo Soetoro was from Indonesia, and Barack Obama later remembered him as having "good manners and easy grace."[4] Lolo and Ann dated for about two years. During that time, Lolo sometimes played chess with Mr. Dunham or wrestled with the young Barry. Then, Ann gave her son big news: Lolo wanted to marry her and the three of them would move to Indonesia.

Lolo went first, and young Barry and his mother reached Jakarta, the capital of Indonesia, in 1967. Lolo took them to their new home. Some of the houses nearby were simple huts, and the neighborhood had only recently gotten electricity. Lolo showed Barry the animals in the backyard. A small ape sat on a tree, and colorful birds walked amidst ducks and chickens. In a small pond, two baby crocodiles sat in the water. Lolo also introduced his stepson to new foods: "dog meat (tough), snake meat (tougher), and roasted grasshopper (crunchy)."[5]

In the months to come, young Barry began to learn more about his new home. Indonesia has many Muslims, followers of the religion Islam. But it also has followers of Asian religions, such as Buddhism and Hinduism. Christians also live there, and Barry entered a Roman Catholic school. Later he went to a Muslim school. Despite these many faiths all around them, neither Lolo nor Ann were very religious. Ann taught Barry that "religion was…one of many ways—and not necessarily the best way—

that man attempted to control the unknowable and understand the deeper truths about our lives."[6] He learned about the different faiths, but did not practice any of them, though he was expected to say prayers in school.

SOME TOUGH TIMES

Life was not always easy for young Barry in his new home. He struggled to learn Indonesian, and because he was darker and larger than the other kids, they often teased him. He was also excitable and full of energy, and sometimes his classmates would tie him up to the flagpole in the schoolyard. Still, Barry made friends and played soccer with them. He joined the Boy Scouts, and in class he impressed his teachers. One recalled that he was always willing to help others. Another remembered a paper Barry wrote when he was in third grade. She said he "wrote he wanted to be president. He didn't say what country he wanted to be president of. But he wanted to make everybody happy."[7]

Young Barry's school day actually began hours before he headed off to class. As he later wrote, "Five days a week she [his mother] came into my room at four in the morning, force-fed me breakfast, and proceeded to teach me my English lessons for three hours…"[8] His mother also brought home books about famous African Americans for Barry to read. He learned about the Reverend Martin Luther King Jr. and the civil

"She believed that people were all basically the same under their skin… and that the goal was then to treat everybody as unique individuals."
—Barack Obama

rights movement. Barry's mother wanted him to be proud of his African roots. She also wanted him to understand the difficulties blacks often faced in the United States. Yet she had another important message. As Obama later said, "She believed that people were all basically the same under their skin…and that the goal was then to treat everybody as unique individuals."[9]

During young Barry's time in Jakarta, his stepfather Lolo took on a new job that paid well. The family moved to a nicer house. But his mother began to worry that Indonesia was not the right place for him. She thought he was not getting the best education he could. When Barry accidentally cut his arm one day, his mother took him to the hospital. The doctors, though, seemed more interested in playing dominoes than treating Barry's wound. That incident added to his mother's concerns. With Barry just turning 10, Ann decided to send him back to Hawaii to go to school. ❖

Recalling the Past

In his first book, *Dreams from My Father*, published in 1995, Obama described a moment in Indonesia when he first thought about what it meant to be black in the United States. He saw a magazine article about an African American who used chemicals to try to lighten his skin. The man wanted to look more like a white person. The chemicals had given him an unnatural, ghostly look. The young boy read that thousands of African Americans had paid for this same treatment because they wanted to appear white. The adult Obama recalled how he "felt my face and neck get hot….Seeing that article was violent for me, an ambush attack."[10] Barry finally realized the impact racism had on some blacks. They did not feel free to be themselves, because white people had so much power over their lives. Barry began to notice that few blacks were shown on TV shows or in magazines. His mother's view of the world, he realized, "was somehow incomplete."[11] Young Barry grew more aware of racism in the years to come.

HEADLINES FROM OBAMA'S TEEN YEARS

Here are some major news stories from the time.

Price of Oil Continues to Rise

December 23, 1973 – Tehran, Iran

The Organization of Petroleum Exporting Countries (OPEC) has raised its prices again, following an earlier increase in October. Oil is now about 400 percent more expensive than it was before the first increase. OPEC's members include several Arab countries that are among the world's leading producers of petroleum. Also called oil, petroleum is used to make gasoline, other fuels, and many chemicals. The price increases and OPEC's refusal to sell oil to certain nations, including the United States, are a protest against **Western** support for Israel in its recent war with Egypt. OPEC's actions have led to much higher fuel prices in countries that rely on OPEC oil.

Nixon Resigns

August 9, 1974 – Washington D.C.

President Richard Nixon stepped down today at noon, and Vice President Gerald Ford was then sworn in as the 38th president of the United States. Nixon is the first president ever to resign. Announcing his plan yesterday, Nixon said, "I deeply regret any injuries that may have been done in the course of the events that led to this decision."[1] The U.S. House of Representatives was preparing for his impeachment, a legal process that could have removed him from office. Nixon was accused of committing crimes connected to the Watergate affair. In June 1972, burglars working for Nixon's staff had tried to break into the headquarters of the rival Democratic Party. The office was in Washington's Watergate building. When the burglary was discovered, Nixon tried to cover up his staff's ties to the crime. He then lied about his role in this cover-up.

Last Americans Leave South Vietnam, Ending U.S. Involvement in Vietnam War

April 30, 1975

Americans board a U.S. Marine helicopter, in a rush to flee Vietnam. This exit came soon after the fall of South Vietnam's capital, Saigon, to troops from Communist North Vietnam.

South African Police Kill Black Youths Protesting the Country's Racist Policies

June 16, 1976

Thatcher Chosen Prime Minister

May 4, 1979 – London, England

Margaret Thatcher made history today, becoming the first woman ever to serve as Britain's prime minister. Under the British political system, the prime minister is the head of the government. He or she is chosen from the party that holds the most seats in Parliament, which makes laws for the country. Thatcher has promised to lower taxes and reduce government spending. After her victory, she said, "Now that the election is over, may we get together and strive to serve and strengthen the country of which we're so proud to be a part."[2]

Americans Taken Hostage in Iranian Capital of Tehran

November 4, 1979

Education of a Young Man

Back in Hawaii, ten-year-old Barry Obama moved in with his grandparents. Their life in Honolulu had changed since 1967. The Dunhams had moved from a house to a much smaller apartment. Stanley now sold life insurance, and Madelyn had worked her way up at the bank and become a vice president. Reaching that level was rare for a woman at the time in Hawaii, when men controlled most important jobs in banking. To Barry, Madelyn was "Toot"—a shortened version of tutu, *the Hawaiian word for "grandmother."*

With help from Stanley's boss, young Barry received a scholarship to Punahou Academy, one of the best private schools in Hawaii.[1] Entering the fifth grade, he felt a little out of place at first. The kids didn't play the games he had played in Indonesia, such as soccer and chess. And he, as he later wrote, "had no idea how to throw a football in a spiral or balance on a skateboard."[2] Slowly, though, Barry made a few friends and adjusted to life in Hawaii.

His first Christmas back in the United States was a special one. His mother and half-sister Maya came from Indonesia for the holidays, and his father also visited. His mom arrived a few weeks before Barack Obama Sr. did. She told Barry about Kenya and the Obamas' tribe, the Luo.

Obama's Tribe

Young Barry read books about the Luo. He was disappointed to learn that they lived in huts and raised cattle. He had imagined them building huge pyramids, as the ancient Egyptians had. Later he learned that some Luo were successful farmers and fishers. The Luo live in parts of Tanzania and Uganda as well as Kenya. About 13 percent of Kenya's population belongs to the tribe. Most Luo in Kenya live near Lake Victoria, while others live in the capital, Nairobi. The Luo and other tribes in Kenya have sometimes fought for control of the country's government. Violence between the Luo and another tribe erupted after disputed elections in 2007.[3]

"If my father hadn't disappointed me, he remained something unknown... and [a little] threatening."
—Barack Obama

BARRY MEETS HIS FATHER

Young Barry had no memories of his father from his early childhood. When he finally met him, he was surprised at how thin his father was. He later learned that his father had a new wife in Africa, and Barry had several half-brothers and half-sisters there.

Barack Obama Sr. stayed in Hawaii for about one month. He visited young Barry's school to speak about Kenya. Barry feared the other kids might make fun of him, if his father talked about the Luo's simple lives. But Senior's tales of hunting lions and Kenya's fight to win its independence from Great Britain impressed the students.[4]

After the visit, young Barry had mixed feelings about his father. "If my father hadn't disappointed me," he later wrote, "he remained something unknown…and [a little] threatening."[5] But his father did give him a special memory. Just before he left for Kenya, Senior danced and laughed to a record of African music, urging his son to dance with him. Barry never forgot that moment—the last time he would see his father alive.

Barack Obama Sr. also gave Barry his first basketball. Barry began to practice dribbling and shooting, and the sport soon became his greatest

Barry and Barack Obama Sr. at the Honolulu airport during his month long visit to the United States. Little did he know that it would be the last time he would see his father.

interest. By the time he reached high school, Barry was good enough to play on the school team. His teammates called him "Barry O'Bomber," because he liked to shoot far away from the basket. His coach later recalled that Barry "practiced hard…he practiced at the 10 a.m. juice break; he practiced at the lunch break at noon; and he was the last one to leave each day."[6]

Still, even with Barry's hard work, the coach didn't think he was good enough to start for the team. Barry also sometimes questioned the coach's style of play. Barry thought the team should play at a faster pace—the kind of basketball he liked. The coach did not change his mind. Once he and Barry got into an argument, and the coach refused to play him for several games.[7] When he wasn't with the school team, Barry found plenty of playing time in informal games on the playgrounds.

HIGH SCHOOL YEARS

About a year after young Barry returned to Hawaii, his mother and sister came back there to live. Ann had separated from Lolo, and they later divorced. Ann, Barry, and his sister lived together in a small apartment. She later decided to return to college to pursue a degree in anthropology—the study of how different peoples live. A few years later, when Barry was about 14 and in high school, she left to do research in Indonesia. Ann took Maya with her. Barry stayed in Hawaii with his grandparents, where he had friends and a life he enjoyed.

"I learned to slip back and forth between my black and white worlds, understanding that each possessed its own languages and customs…"
—Barack Obama

Through high school, Barry was mostly a B student. Although focused on basketball, he also enjoyed writing poetry and singing in the chorus. For a time, he worked in an ice cream shop, though he grew to dislike ice cream. He preferred a local sweet treat—shaved ice covered with fruit-flavored syrup.

Outside of class, Barry had several groups of friends. They enjoyed body surfing as the Pacific Ocean rolled onto the island shores. Others played basketball with Barry. Sometimes they drank beer or smoked marijuana. At the time, the drinking age in the United States was 18, so it was illegal for Barry to drink. Smoking marijuana was also against the law. But Barry and his friends ignored the laws. Starting in the 1960s, some teens chose to try illegal drugs. They wanted to rebel against their parents or assert their independence. Some used drugs because they were going through hard times at home or school. Obama later wrote that the drugs and alcohol helped him escape from thinking about who he was and blurred "the edges of my memory."[8] Later in life, though, he stopped using drugs and rarely drank. He called his earlier drug use a bad decision.

At Punahou, most of the students were white, and many came from wealthy families. Some others were Asian. Barry was one of the few black or mixed-race students. He got along with everyone. He sometimes met with other students who were black or racially mixed. They called themselves the "Ethnic Corner." He also had some white friends. He later wrote, "I learned to slip back and forth between my black and white worlds, understanding that each possessed its own languages and customs…"[9]

EXAMINING HIS RACIAL ROOTS

At times, he began to think more about his African roots. Some of his African American friends told him that white people held power over blacks; they set the rules. Yet some whites, even his own grandmother,

Barack Obama in his high school yearbook, 1979.

also feared blacks. The whites thought African Americans might harm them. Barry wanted to learn more about what it was like to be black in the United States. He began to read books by famous African American authors, such as Ralph Ellison and Langston Hughes. Most of his friends never realized how much time Barry spent trying to understand what it meant to be both black and white.

"With the right words everything could change—South Africa, the lives of the ghetto kids just a few miles away, my own [uncertain] place in the world."
—Barack Obama

Barry graduated from Punahou Academy in May 1979. During the summer, he turned 18, and that fall he headed to Occidental College, in Los Angeles, California. The school had offered him a scholarship. For the first time in his life, Barry lived on the mainland of the United States. And soon, for the first time, he began to use his real first name—Barack. Barack became friends with other black students on the campus. He often talked about world events and race with them, and with white friends as well. He also showed his first public interest in politics. At the time, South Africa was filled with racial tension. A small number of whites controlled the government and the economy, and they strictly limited the rights of the country's black citizens. The racial system there was called **apartheid**. In the United States, the United Kingdom, and other parts of the world, thousands of people and groups protested business dealings with South African companies. The protestors wanted to stop any money from going to South Africa if it was helping to support apartheid.

Barack took part in a rally calling for Occidental's trustees to pull any money or investments out of South Africa. He was supposed to say

Roots and the Search for Roots

Barack Obama did not make his first trip to Kenya until his late 20's. But during the 1970s, many African Americans were thinking about the homeland of their ancestors, because of the TV show *Roots*. The eight-part series was based on a book by Alex Haley. He blended truth and fiction to tell the story of his family, starting with a Muslim tribesman named Kunta Kinte. During the 1760s, slave traders captured Kinte and brought him to America. Millions of Americans, black and white, watched *Roots* the mini-series, and it remains one of the most popular TV shows of all time. The show led to greater study of African American history in schools and discussions about race. Some African Americans also began to research their own roots, looking for information about ancestors who were slaves.[10]

a few words to start the rally. "With the right words," he later wrote, "everything could change—South Africa, the lives of the ghetto kids just a few miles away, my own [uncertain] place in the world."[11] As he spoke, some of the students gathered around him began to clap and cheer. "I knew that I had them, that the connection had been made."[12]

HEADING TO NEW YORK

After two years at Occidental, Barack transferred to Columbia University in New York City. Columbia is part of the "Ivy League"—eight of the oldest and best colleges in the United States. Before heading to New York, he traveled with a friend to Indonesia, so Barack could see his mother and sister. The two young men also spent time in Pakistan visiting the family of one of Barack's college friends.

At Columbia, Barack studied harder than he had in high school or at

Occidental. He no longer did drugs and began to exercise regularly, running three miles every day.[13] He also continued to explore African American culture and new political ideas. One fellow classmate said that Barack was more mature than most students at Columbia. "He was our age, but seemed older because of his poise."[14]

In 1982, just a few months after Barack turned 21, he received a phone call with some bad news. His father had died in a car crash in Kenya. Barack did not go to the funeral. And as he wrote in *Dreams from My Father*, almost a year passed before he finally cried over Senior's death. He reread letters his father had sent him. Years later he would go to Kenya to try to learn more about the father he had never really known.

> ### *"I had an obligation to take not only my own talents more seriously but also see what I could contribute to others."*
> —Barack Obama

During his last year of college, Barack decided that he wanted to be a community organizer, a person who helps local residents make changes in their community. He was inspired by the civil rights movement and the belief that America needed to change to help all its citizens lead better lives. Barack believed that "change won't come from the top" and "communities had to be created, fought for, tended like gardens."[15] He sent letters to groups and political leaders that shared his goals, but none of them offered him a job. Still, the idea of helping others was strong. During his college years, Barack later said, he realized for the first time that "I had an obligation to take not only my own talents more seriously but also see what I could contribute to others."[16] ❖

In a few years, Barack would visit his family in Kenya for the first time. This is a picture from that visit in 1987. He is with his grandmother, Sarah. The picture is from his grandmother's collection.

Headlines from Obama's Early Chicago Years

Here are some major news stories from the time.

Guion Bluford, Aboard Space Shuttle *Challenger*, Becomes First African American in Space

August 30, 1983

Terrorist Bombs Kill Marines, French Troops

Beirut, Lebanon – October 23, 1983

A bomb blast at the U.S. base at Beirut International Airport killed 241 Marines. Just moments later, a second attack on a nearby French base killed 58 soldiers. In each blast, a **terrorist** who drove a truck filled with explosives also died. The Marines and French troops were part of an international force sent to Lebanon to try to end fighting between competing groups in the country. Some of the Lebanese had received support from Israel, while the others were backed by two of Israel's enemies in the region, Syria and Iran. The military base attacks followed an earlier terrorist bomb blast that April, which killed 63 people at the U.S. Embassy in Beirut.

Shuttle *Challenger* Explodes After Liftoff

Cape Canaveral, Florida – January 28, 1986

Just moments after liftoff, the space shuttle *Challenger* exploded. The blast killed all seven crewmembers on board, including Christa McAuliffe. She was the first teacher ever chosen to fly on a shuttle mission. The deadly blast was shown live on television, leaving viewers around the world stunned. President Ronald Reagan said after, "This is truly a national loss…. The crew of the space shuttle *Challenger* honored us by the manner in which they lived their lives."[1]

Deadly Accident at Nuclear Power Plant

Pripyat, Ukraine – April 26, 1986

An explosion and fire at the Chernobyl **nuclear** power plant released large amounts of radiation into the atmosphere. Radiation is a form of energy that, in large doses, can kill humans and wildlife. The radiation from the plant is spreading, posing a risk to people across Europe and the **Soviet Union**. The fire and explosion killed some immediately, dozens of others will die of radiation poisoning within weeks. It is the worst nuclear accident in history.

Worst Storm in Almost Three Centuries Hits Great Britain; Damage Totals £ 1.3 billion ($2.3 billion)

October 16, 1987

Two Leaders Agree to Weapons Cut

Washington, D.C. – December 8, 1987

U.S. President Ronald Reagan and Mikhail Gorbachev, leader of the Soviet Union, reached a historic agreement to reduce nuclear weapons. Both countries will destroy all their missiles able to travel between 500 km (311 miles) and 5,500 km (3,418 miles). Since the end of World War II in 1945, the United States and the Soviet Union have competed to build more and better weapons. This "arms race" is part of the Cold War, the struggle between the two nations to win allies and limit each other's influence around the world. Today's agreement is part of an ongoing effort between the two countries to improve their relations.

In the Community

In 1983, Obama graduated from Columbia with a degree in political science and English literature. Since no one had offered him work as a community organizer, he took a job with the Business International Corporation. The company gave advice to U.S. companies doing business around the world. Obama did research and wrote papers. Within a few months, he had his own office and a secretary. But he was not happy, and he began to search again for a job as a community organizer.

Obama was offered one job, but it involved working with powerful business people and government officials. He wanted a **grassroots** job, working with the people who needed help. Finally, a man named Jerry Kellman called. Obama had answered an ad he placed seeking an organizer. Kellman worked for a group in Chicago that wanted to help black neighborhoods on the city's South Side. That part of Chicago had a large African American population that often struggled to find jobs and good housing. Obama would help Kellman's group try to keep factory jobs in the city.

Obama thought the job was just what he wanted. As he later said, "This was the best opportunity I had to work directly with people….This was, also, trying to organize them so they could take control of their lives…"[1] Obama was ready to give up his well-paying job in New York to fulfill his dream.

Sweet Home Chicago

African Americans first came to Chicago in large numbers during the "Great Migration." This movement of blacks from small Southern towns to cities in the North and Midwest began in the 1890s. The blacks left the rural farming communities in the South seeking abundant and better-paying jobs in factories and plants.

In Chicago, that often meant working in the city's steel mills or **stockyards**. The Great Migration reached its peak between 1915 and 1930, when 1.25 million blacks moved. From 1910 to 1920, Chicago's black population almost tripled. Chicago became a center for black culture. Its musicians helped create modern jazz and blues. Obama had made an earlier visit to Chicago, with his family, in 1972. He saw many of the city's famous sites, including the elevated train tracks, called the el, and the Field Museum. Today the Field is home to Sue, the largest set of Tyrannosaurus Rex bones ever displayed.

NEW CITY, NEW JOB

With money from Kellman's group, Obama bought an old car and headed to Chicago. He arrived in June 1985, not knowing anyone except Kellman. Chicago had a history of segregation—the separation of different races. When Obama arrived, race deeply divided the city's politics. In 1983, voters chose Harold Washington as Chicago's first black mayor. White members on the city council opposed him and his plans. Obama supported Washington, and he knew that his election had made Chicago's black residents proud. But the political division in the city meant the government was not doing much to help the poor.[2]

Kellman put Obama in charge of the Developing Communities Project (DCP). Obama would help people in Roseland, a neighborhood about

32 km (20 miles) south of central Chicago. By the time Obama arrived, many of the residents were living in poverty. Companies that once ran factories in the area had left the city, forcing people out of work. Kellman wanted the people of Roseland to see that they had power to improve their lives, if they worked together.

At first, Obama struggled with his new job. He had to win the trust of the local people, which was not easy for someone just 23 years old. Some of the residents called him "Baby Face Obama."[3] But Obama assured them he was ready to learn and to work hard. He began interviewing people in Roseland to see what issues concerned them most. One was safety: Some people thought the Chicago police ignored their neighborhood. Obama

Chicago is known for its architecture as well as for its placement on the shore of Lake Michigan. Some of the best views of the city must be seen from a boat!

set up a meeting with a local police commander and sent out notices in the neighborhood. He was disappointed when the commander later cancelled and sent a lower-ranking officer instead, and when few people came to the meeting.

Obama thought everyone would want to work together to solve problems. But he soon realized that each neighborhood had ministers and other local leaders who did not want to share whatever power they already had. Obama saw that making many changes quickly would be hard.

Obama focused on winning small gains for the people he served. He began working with the residents of Altgeld Gardens, a housing complex near Roseland. The city was supposed to take care of the buildings, but Obama saw many problems: "Ceilings crumbled. Pipes burst. Toilets backed up."[4] And here, as in Roseland, many people struggled to find good jobs. Obama decided to make jobs one of his first issues at Altgeld.

For two weeks, Obama prepared for a meeting with the Mayor's Office of Employment and Training (MET). The office helped people without jobs get training for new careers. Obama wanted the MET to open an office close to Altgeld Gardens. He and the others in his group worked hard to make sure local people came to the meeting. He did not want to repeat the failure of the first meeting with the police. This time, the meeting went well. The city agreed to the residents' request.

"It needs to be done, and not enough folks are doing it."
—Barack Obama on why he worked as a community organizer

GETTING THINGS DONE

After about a year of working for the Developing Communities Project, Obama began to see the results of his hard work. The residents had convinced the city to improve some services on the Far South Side, such as garbage removal. The city also began to rebuild some parks and playgrounds in the area and fix some roads. Local politicians now knew who Obama was. Some people still wondered why a college-educated person did what he did. One woman said, "The pay is low, the hours is long, and don't nobody appreciate you."[5] Obama later had an answer for why he worked as a community organizer: "It needs to be done, and not enough folks are doing it."[6]

Despite his first successes, Obama wanted to do more. He and the residents he worked with soon had a new issue: asbestos. This material was once widely used in building materials because it is strong and resists fire. Asbestos, however, can also be harmful to humans. Inhaling it can cause lung cancer or other diseases. As the dangers of asbestos became better known, people began removing it from buildings.

Obama saw a small notice in the newspaper that the city of Chicago was looking for a company to remove asbestos. The material was in the management office at Altgeld Gardens. Obama wondered if the harmful substance could be in the apartments there too. Obama and a resident met with a city official, who told them the apartments had been tested. They did not contain asbestos. Obama wanted to see the results of the test. The official said he would provide the report, but after weeks passed, the report never came.

Obama organized a group of residents to go to downtown Chicago, where the main city offices are located. They went to the city's Housing Department, and officials admitted the apartments had not been tested. They agreed to send the department director to Altgeld for a meeting and to begin testing for the asbestos.

That second meeting didn't go smoothly—the housing director and some of the residents argued before anything was settled. But the city did take some steps to reduce the health risks from the asbestos. Still, Obama was disappointed. Some of the people who had come out for his DCP meetings stopped attending. They found it hard to commit their time. And the city did not receive money from the U.S. government that would get rid of the asbestos once and for all.

TIME FOR OTHER INTERESTS

Obama devoted long hours to his job, even though he sometimes felt what he did was not enough to bring real change. But he also found time to enjoy himself. He lived in Hyde Park, the home of the University of Chicago. Hyde Park had more of a mix of blacks and whites than Roseland. It also had bookstores, restaurants, and bars. Obama sometimes played basketball on the local courts or went out with girlfriends. For a time he lived with one of them. His most lasting relationship, however, was with his cat Max. The two of them lived together in a cramped apartment flooded with books.

> *"I loved all the different neighborhoods and all the different ethnic groups I was interacting with."*
> —Barack Obama on his community work

Obama still had a love of words, and he constantly took notes in pads that he always carried with him. At times, he also drew cartoon-like

> **"...ordinary people can do extraordinary things when they're given a chance."**
> —Barack Obama

sketches of the people he met. Writing, though, was his true artistic love.[7] In his apartment, he wrote short stories he hoped to publish in a book. He based some of the characters on the people he met in his new hometown. Obama later said, "I loved all the different neighborhoods and all the different ethnic groups I was interacting with."[8] Obama also loved learning that "ordinary people can do extraordinary things when they're given a chance."[9] The Altgeld Garden residents' effort to challenge city officials and work for change was one example of this.

Not everyone Obama met was ordinary. During an outdoor meeting Obama organized, Emil Jones Jr. stopped by. Jones was an Illinois state senator. Jones thought Obama "was very bright, very intelligent, a little pushy..."[10] Later, Jones would help Obama launch his political career in Illinois.

Obama also met members of his family for the first time. He visited his half-brother Roy in Washington D.C., where he lived. And Obama's half-sister Auma came to see him in Chicago. She had left her native Kenya to study in Germany. She and Obama had talked on the phone before this visit. Auma told stories about Barack Senior and his life in Kenya. He was forced out of a government job because his political views upset some leaders. He struggled to find a good job, and often drank too much alcohol. Barack Senior also had troubles sometimes with his wives and children. Obama saw a true picture of his father and realized, "Whatever I do, it seems, I won't do much worse than you."[11]

Another important new person in Obama's life was Reverend Jeremiah

Wright. Obama met many of the local ministers during his job. But Wright seemed to have more in common with him, as far as intelligence and beliefs about the world.[12] Wright was also more liberal than most of Chicago's black ministers. He supported equal rights for homosexuals, at a time when most U.S. states did not offer them legal protection from discrimination. Wright also spoke out on other political issues, such as civil rights for blacks. In many African American churches, members sometimes looked to their ministers for direction on many issues, not just religious concerns.

Through his job, Obama saw the importance of the churches in the black neighborhoods. For decades, they had played a key role in black communities. The religious message of Christianity offered hope for a better life in heaven. And the ministers also helped people deal with the problems of the present. Obama saw, he later said, "the power of [the black] church to give people courage against great odds. And it moved me deeply."[13]

"[Obama] was very bright, very intelligent, a little pushy…"
—Illinois state senator Emil Jones Jr.

Obama decided to attend Wright's church, Trinity United Church of Christ. Sometime in 1987 or 1988, Reverend Wright asked if anyone in the church wanted to walk down to the altar and devote themselves to Christ. Obama rose and said he did. Obama had been exposed to different religious beliefs his whole life. Now, for the first time, he freely called himself a Christian.[14]

"...there was something more than making money and getting a fancy degree. The measure of my life would be public service."
—Barack Obama

Along with his new faith, Obama began to sense that he could do more to help others. After meetings, he left thinking the city's politicians and lawyers knew more than he did. They could find ways to fight the changes he sought. In the fall of 1987, he told a friend, "I just can't get things done here without a law degree. I've got to get a law degree to work against these guys..."[15] Earlier, Obama attended a conference at Harvard. He thought about his father attending the school decades before. He decided that he would go there to study law.

In 1988, now approaching his 27th birthday, Obama left his job at DCP and said goodbye to his friends. Years later, he told other DCP workers that his time organizing made him realize "there was something more than making money and getting a fancy degree. The measure of my life would be public service."[16] But before moving to Massachusetts, Obama wanted to take an important trip. ❖

Hyde Park

With a vibrant mix of people and the esteemed University of Chicago, Hyde Park is one of Chicago's most interesting neighborhoods. It's the home of several museums, including the DuSable Museum of African American History and the Museum of Science and Industry, whose impressive building was originally built by architect Daniel Burnham for the 1893 World's Fair. It is the only building from the fair that remains. Buildings and homes by architects such as Mies van der Rohe, Frank Lloyd Wright, and I.M. Pei, can all be found in this historic neighborhood.

Headlines from Obama's Harvard Years and Return to Chicago

Here are some major news stories from the time.

Chinese Army Kill Protesters in Beijing's Tiananmen Square

June 3, 1989

The Chinese army opened fire on democratic protesters, killing hundreds. This photo of a student protester putting himself directly in harm's way has become one of the most famous photos ever taken. It is now seen as a symbol for the power of protest.

The Berlin Wall Opens

West Berlin, West Germany –
November 9, 1989

East German guards opened gates along the Berlin Wall, allowing East Berliners to freely travel to the West for the first time in 28 years. The Berlin Wall has long been a symbol of the Cold War. This struggle for influence between the United States and its allies against the **Communist** governments of the Soviet Union and Eastern Europe began after World War II. In 1961, with Soviet permission, East Germany built the Berlin Wall. East German officials wanted to prevent their citizens from seeking jobs, goods, and freedom in West Germany. Now, Soviet officials are letting their allies in East Germany introduce greater political freedom. With the opening of the Berlin Wall, many Germans hope their two countries will be reunited.

Operation Desert Storm a Success

Washington, DC –
February 27, 1991

After just four days of battle, international forces have driven Iraqi troops out of Kuwait. U.S. and British forces led the assault, known as Operation Desert Storm. The fighting actually began almost six weeks ago, when U.S. and British planes bombed targets across Iraq. Iraqi leader Saddam Hussein had sparked the conflict in August 1990, when he invaded neighboring Kuwait and refused to leave. U.S. President George Bush led the international effort to force Saddam's troops from Kuwait. After the fighting ended, Bush said, "This is a victory for all mankind, for the rule of law, and for what is right."[1]

Toni Morrison Wins Nobel Prize for Literature; First African American So Honored

October 7, 1993

Harvard and Back

After traveling for a few weeks through Europe, Barack Obama sat on a plane heading for Nairobi, the capital of Kenya. In Kenya, he hoped to learn more about his father and better understand his own life. His sister Auma met him at the airport, along with their aunt, their father's sister.

Obama soon met other members of his large family. Barack Senior had fathered children with three other women besides Ann Dunham. All together, Obama had eight half-brothers and sisters, including Maya. One of the brothers had died before Obama made his trip to Kenya. During his stay, Obama met some of these half-siblings as well as other family members for the first time. They told him tales of his father and grandfather.

From Nairobi, Obama traveled with Auma into the wild on a safari. He saw zebra, gazelles, wildebeests, and other animals that roam the plains of Kenya. Obama also went to the small town of Alego, where his grandfather had owned land and where his father was born. His grandfather Onyango had worked for the British in Nairobi, and during World War II he traveled with a British officer to Asia. When he returned to Kenya, he settled in Alego and began farming. Obama learned that his grandfather was a strict man, and his father was a clever boy who sometimes got into trouble.

After hearing the tales, Barack imagined what his grandfather and father had been like long ago, before he was born. He thought about their struggles to improve their lives. He sat by their graves, which were in the backyard of the family's house. He cried, thinking about these two men he had never known, but who had shaped his life. As he later wrote, "I saw that my life in America—the black life, the white life, the sense of abandonment I'd felt as a boy, the frustration and hope I'd witnessed in Chicago—all of it was connected with this small plot of earth an ocean away…"[1]

ACHIEVEMENTS IN LAW SCHOOL

Obama spent a few more weeks in Kenya, then returned to Chicago. From there, he drove to Cambridge, home of Harvard University. This time, no one was paying his way; he had to take out loans for law school. Harvard, like Columbia, was an Ivy League school, and its law school was one of the best in the United States. Many graduates went on to make large salaries at top law firms. Obama, though, wanted to use his law degree to help others. He also considered running for a political office one day.

> ### *"…most amazing research assistant."*
> —Lawrence Tribe, Harvard professor

Obama stood out among the students at Harvard. Most went to law school right after earning their first college degrees. Many came from wealthy families. At 27, he was older than most of the other students. He had also seen different cultures, thanks to his time in Indonesia and Kenya. And as one of only 180 blacks out of about 1,600 students, he had greater experience of the role of race in America.

During his first year, Obama spent long hours in the library. He also did research for one of the school's top professors, Lawrence Tribe. Tribe said that Obama was his "most amazing research assistant."[2] Obama worked on a wide range of issues, including legal debates over abortion.

Thanks to his high grades and good relationship with Tribe and other professors, Obama was chosen to be one of the editors for the *Harvard Law Review*. Students produced the journal to stir debate on current legal issues. The *Review* was and is still the most important legal publication in the country.[3] After one year at Harvard, Obama was showing his talents and impressing others.

MEETING AN IMPORTANT NEW PERSON

In the summer of 1989, Obama traveled back to Chicago to work at one of the city's most famous law firms. He was an intern, which meant he earned little or no pay, but he got the chance to learn how law is actually practiced. When he arrived at the firm, he was teamed up with a young lawyer, Michelle Robinson. She was one of the few black attorneys there. When she first heard about Obama and his background she thought, "On paper we couldn't be more different....I thought he was going to be weird."[4]

> *"…Barack stood up that day, and…talked about the world as it is, and the world as it should be. And he said that all too often, we accept the distance between the two."*
> —Michelle Robinson

But Robinson and Obama had some things in common. She had gone to an Ivy League school, as he had. She had also gone to Harvard Law, graduating in 1988. She was tall, intelligent, and confident.[5] The two soon spent time together outside of the office. On their first date, they went to see a movie by Spike Lee, a black filmmaker. Others dates

The Obamas on their wedding day, October 18th, 1992. When they married, Barack was 31 years old and Michelle was 27.

soon followed. Robinson took Obama to meet her family, who lived in Chicago. On the basketball court, he impressed her brother Craig, who had been a star player in college. Obama also talked about his future with Craig, saying at some point he'd like to run for office—maybe even president some day.

On another date, Obama took Robinson to visit a church to meet some people he knew from his work in Chicago. As she later said, "...Barack

Spike Lee's Powerful Pictures

Since the 1980s, Spike Lee has been one of the most famous black filmmakers in Hollywood. His films, such as *Do the Right Thing* (1989), have often dealt with the relations between whites and blacks. This movie was the one Barack Obama and Michelle Robinson saw on their first date. Lee has also made action movies and shot commercials. One of his movies was about the life of Malcolm X. During the 1960s, Malcolm X had spoken out strongly against racism and for the rights of African Americans. As a teen, Obama had read Malcolm X's life story. Alex Haley, the author of *Roots*, wrote the book based on interviews with Malcolm X. Obama related to Malcolm's experience of having both white and black relatives, as Malcolm's grandfather was white. Obama later used some of Malcolm X's writing when he taught law.

stood up that day, and…talked about the world as it is, and the world as it should be. And he said that all too often, we accept the distance between the two."[6] Obama wanted to create the world as it should be, with better lives for everyone. This view impressed Robinson, even as she realized he would probably never make much money. At the time, she said, Obama wore "cruddy" clothes and his car had a hole in the door where it had rusted away. "You could see the ground when you were driving," she later said.[7]

MAKING HISTORY FOR THE FIRST TIME

Returning to Harvard that fall, Obama was in love with Robinson, and they kept in touch often. Obama juggled his studies with his work on the *Law Review*. Early in 1990, he announced he was a candidate for the presidency of the journal, one of 19 people seeking the title. That position often leads to jobs with important judges and a powerful legal career. Obama had not wanted to run at first, since he knew he did not want that kind of career. Plus, he knew no black student had ever been chosen president. His friends, however, convinced him to try. Obama recalled that one black friend told him, "'That is a door that needs to be kicked down, and you can take it down.'"[8]

Some of the editors on the *Review* had conflicting political and legal views. A large number were liberal, but some were conservative. Obama was liberal, with his support of civil rights and other issues that called for the government to play a role in ensuring equality. But he also got along well with the conservatives at Harvard. One later said that Obama "always floated a little bit above those controversies and divisions…He was a more mature and more reasonable and more open-minded person."[9]

The voting for the new president went on for hours. At the end, some of the conservatives backed Obama over another liberal. One said, "Whatever his politics, we felt he would give us a fair shake."[10] Before the final vote was announced, another black editor rushed up to greet him. He grabbed Obama and hugged him. Obama later wrote, "It was

> *"[Obama] always floated a little bit above those controversies and divisions… He was a more mature and more reasonable and more open-minded person."*
> —a conservative editor at
> the *Harvard Law Review*

then that I knew it was more than just about me. It was about us [blacks at Harvard]."[11]

Obama's historic election as the first black president of the *Harvard Law Review* quickly became national news. *The New York Times*, one of the most important U.S. newspapers, interviewed him, as did other papers and magazines. Harvard's Professor Tribe praised Obama in one important newspaper, saying, "He's able to build upon what others say and see what's valuable in their comments without belittling them."[12] A book publisher gave him a contract to write about his experience at Harvard. Obama missed his deadline for writing that book, and the publisher cancelled the contract. But Obama soon had another deal, which led to his writing *Dreams from My Father*.

Although Obama got along well with everyone, white and black, racial tensions were high at Harvard. At the time, the law school had few African American professors. One of these professors and some black students wanted the school to do more to hire African Americans and women. Obama supported the effort to hire more blacks, but he did not play an active role in a legal protest some students supported.

Obama also did not always agree with some of the black law students on other issues. Some thought he did not give enough black students important jobs at the law review. They also believed he gave too many jobs to conservative editors. But Obama wanted to balance the different

Barack Obama on campus at Harvard Law School. This photo was taken after he was elected president of the Harvard Law Review *in 1990. He graduated in 1991.*

views of the editors. And despite the arguments that sometimes arose, he made most of the editors see the need to work for a common goal.[13] One black editor later said, "Barack was the one who was truly able to move between the different groups."[14]

NEW RESPONSIBILITIES

Running the *Harvard Law Review* was like a full-time job, and sometimes Obama missed his classes. He was also still deeply involved with Michelle Robinson. She wanted to get married, and for a time Obama resisted. Finally, in 1991, he asked her to marry him. That year, Obama also received his law degree, and he moved back to Chicago.

The next year was busy for Obama. He began teaching law at the University of Chicago. And before starting a job at a Chicago law firm, he ran a non-profit group called Project Vote! It tried to recruit people to register to vote. Project Vote! targeted blacks and other minorities in Cook County, where Chicago is located. Historically, not as many of those people had registered to vote as wealthier whites did. The minorities might not have understood the process or thought that voting was not important. Obama and his staff tried to convince these residents that they should register and vote. Many people did register, in part because an African American named Carol Moseley Braun was running for office. A member of the Democratic Party, Braun hoped to be one of Illinois's two U.S. senators.

Braun won the election, becoming the first black female ever in the Senate. Political experts gave Obama and Project Vote! credit for attracting new voters that helped her win.[15] Obama saw the value of getting blacks to vote. Political leaders in Chicago would now have to pay more attention to their concerns. If not, the leaders would lose their votes. Obama said, "We plan to hold politicians' feet to the flames in 1993, to remind them that we can produce a bloc of voters large enough that it cannot be ignored."[16]

As 1993 began, Obama was preparing for his job at a Chicago law firm while still teaching part-time. He and Michelle had married the previous October, and Obama was ready to begin the next phase of his life. ❖

Nelson Mandela is the First Black President of South Africa

When Obama began work for his new job at the law firm, one of the biggest news stories of the time was the build-up to South Africa's multi-racial elections in 1994.

Since 1948, South Africa had been under apartheid, which was a system of laws enforcing racial segregation that greatly favored the white minority.

Nelson Mandela spent 27 years in prison for being an anti-apartheid activist and for leading the militant wing of the African National Congress (ANC), an anti-apartheid political party. He was released from prison in 1990 by F.W. de Klerk, the president of the National Party (which supported apartheid).

Seeing that his party was losing international support, de Klerk decided to hold South Africa's first multi-racial elections. The ANC's candidate was Nelson Mandela. He won the election and was sworn in on May 10, 1994.

Nelson Mandela celebrates winning his country's first multi-racial election.

HEADLINES FROM OBAMA'S TIME IN THE ILLINOIS SENATE

Here are some major news stories from the time.

Agreement Reached to End War in Former Yugoslavia

Dayton, Ohio – November 21, 1995

The leaders of Serbia, Croatia, and Bosnia have agreed to terms that will end fighting in their countries. All three were once part of Yugoslavia, which began splitting into independent republics in 1991. The division unleashed age-old ethnic and religious disputes, as different groups tried to assert control in the new republics. Troops from the North Atlantic Treaty Organization (NATO) will be sent to Bosnia to help keep the peace. NATO members include the United States, Canada, Great Britain, France, Germany, and Italy.

Estimated 2.5 Billion Viewers Watch Funeral for Beloved Princess Diana

September 6, 1997

Hillary Clinton Wins U.S. Senate Seat; Becomes First Former First Lady to Hold National Elected Office

November 7, 2000

Supreme Court Rules in Favor of Bush

Washington D. C. – December 12, 2000

On a 5-4 vote, the U.S. Supreme Court ruled that Florida must stop recounting votes cast in the recent presidential election between George W. Bush and Vice President Al Gore. The ruling means that an earlier recount giving Bush a win in the state will stand. The popular vote was extremely close in Florida, and Gore had argued that some voters had been confused by the ballots used in the state. Also, some voting machines may not have worked properly. By taking Florida and its 27 **electoral votes**, Bush has a total of 271—just one more electoral vote than he needed to become the 43rd U.S. president.

Terrorist Attack Kills Almost 3,000

New York City – September 11, 2001

See page 65.

Plane Safely Diverted After Man Onboard Discovered with Explosives in Shoe

December 22, 2001

Escorted by F-15 fighter jets, American Airlines Flight 63, from Paris to Miami, made an emergency landing at Boston Logan International Airport after it was discovered that a man onboard was trying to ignite a bomb in his shoe. Flight attendants and passengers subdued the man with plastic handcuffs, seatbelts, and headphone cords. The suspected terrorist, London-born Richard Reid was immediately arrested upon landing.

The Obamas settled into a condo in Hyde Park. Michelle now worked for the city of Chicago, and Barack began practicing law at Davis, Miner, Barnhill & Galland. The firm mostly worked for people who believed others had denied them their civil rights or treated them unfairly at work. Obama did not go to court; instead, he worked behind the scenes, doing research for trials and lawsuits.

At night, he spent long hours at home working on *Dreams from My Father*. He also had his courses to teach at the University of Chicago. In his spare time, he still enjoyed playing basketball, and sometimes he and Michelle went to the movies or out to dinner.

In the summer of 1995, Obama finally published his book. Just a few months later, he received bad news: His mother had died of cancer. The disease had spread quickly, and Obama did not have one last chance to say goodbye. He later regretted this, and said, "she was the kindest, most generous spirit I have ever known."[1] Ann Dunham's thoughts on politics had shaped Obama's own. Like her, he was a Democrat. More so than the rival Republicans, the Democrats support using the government's powers to shape the economy and promote equality for its citizens.

> *"she was the kindest, most generous spirit I have ever known."*
> —Barack Obama

SERVING IN THE ILLINOIS SENATE

Around the time of his mother's death, Obama began his first political **campaign**. He ran for a seat in the Illinois state senate. In Chicago politics, Democrats greatly outnumber Republicans and usually win easily. The real race is often the **primary** between several Democrats seeking to win the party's **nomination** for a particular seat as a senator. Obama won a legal battle that said his opponents had not followed the rules for putting their names on the ballot. With that legal victory, Obama won his first political election.

Making Laws

In the United States, lawmakers work at both the state and national levels. A body that makes laws is called the legislature. The national legislature, the U.S. Congress, has two parts, the House of Representatives and the Senate. Each state receives a set number of representatives, based on its population. The House has a total of 435 representatives. Each House member represents a geographic area called a district. Each of the 50 states also elects two senators, and each represents the interests of the entire state. Every state except Nebraska also has a legislature divided into a House and Senate. Both representatives and senators represent districts within their state.

> *"Our goal must be to help
> people get a sense of building
> something larger....People are
> hungry for community; they miss it.
> They are hungry for change."*
> —Barack Obama

Before the vote, he had discussed some of his ideas about politics and society. Many Americans, he said, stressed the individual too much. Some problems had to be solved by people coming together as a community. "Our goal must be to help people get a sense of building something larger....People are hungry for community; they miss it. They are hungry for change."[2]

At 34 years old and now a state senator, Obama's life became busier than ever. He spent part of his time in Springfield, the capital of Illinois. When he wasn't considering new laws for the state, he was teaching or working at his law firm. Since state lawmakers were not paid highly, Obama decided to teach more classes at the University of Chicago. Most students enjoyed him, calling him one of the best teachers at the school. His most popular class was about racism and the law. Obama freely talked about his own experiences as a black man and challenged students to look at their own ideas on race. One former student said that Obama also "wanted his students to consider the impact laws and judicial opinions had on real people."[3]

In Springfield, Obama tried to bring that concern to the laws he helped write. His first few years in the Senate were not easy. Some people thought he could be arrogant and unfriendly.[4] Also, the Republicans controlled the Senate at the time, so Democrats could not easily pass the laws they wanted. Obama saw the value in trying to work with

Republicans in order to get things done. He learned to play golf, since the lawmakers often talked politics while they played. He also played poker with some senators so he could build friendships.

> *"…in the faces of all the men and women I'd met I had recognized pieces of myself…. Not so far beneath the surface, I think, we are becoming more, not less alike."*
> —Barack Obama

In the summer of 1997, Obama and an aide took a tour of Illinois. Obama wanted to learn about the problems and concerns of people outside of Chicago. In his second book, *The Audacity of Hope*, published in 2006, he wrote that "in the faces of all the men and women I'd met I had recognized pieces of myself….Not so far beneath the surface, I think, we are becoming more, not less alike."[5]

The leader of the Democrats in the Illinois Senate was Emil Jones Jr. The man who Obama had met years before on the South Side of Chicago now helped him in Springfield. Jones put Obama in charge of a **bill** that would limit the money political candidates received. The goal was to keep wealthy people from gaining favors from lawmakers. The bill passed in 1998—Obama's first success in the Senate. Obama said the new law "communicates [to voters] …that we in fact are willing to do the right thing."[6] All together, during his first two years Obama sponsored (supported) 14 bills that became law. He sponsored even more after that, including some relating to health. One law set aside money to screen for cancer and another provided training in the use of equipment used to treat heart attacks.

During this time, the Obamas became parents for the first time. Their daughter Malia was born on July 4, 1998. Obama soon had to balance two strong desires. He wanted to do all his jobs well, and he also wanted to be a good father. Having grown up without a father, he was determined "that my own children would have a father they could count on."[7] He promised to spend as much time as possible with his family when he was in Chicago.

> *"We [blacks] have more in common with the Latino community, the white community, than we have differences, and you have to work with them..."*
> —Barack Obama

LEARNING A POLITICAL LESSON

Still, Obama was eager to move up to a more important political office. In September 1999, he ran for the U.S. House of Representatives. He challenged the sitting representative, Bobby Rush, a Democrat. Rush, an African American, was not particularly active in the House, but he was well liked by black voters.[8] Some whites, in the district, however, thought he ignored white neighborhoods.[9]

Obama thought he could do a better job representing everyone in Rush's district, which included Hyde Park. Rush, in return, called Obama an "educated fool."[10] He and some voters in the district were not impressed with Obama's Harvard education. As he campaigned, Obama tried to show voters he did not take himself too seriously. He joked about his name, saying people often didn't say *Obama* right. "They say 'Alabama' or 'Yo mama'."[11] Some of his opponents said Obama was more interested in helping whites than the many blacks in the district. Obama said, "We [blacks] have more in common with the Latino community, the white community, than we have differences, and you have to work with them…"[12]

Obama won the support of some wealthy white voters in the district. But the area had more blacks, and they strongly supported Rush. As the campaign went on, Obama knew he was going to lose. He woke up each morning with dread, "realizing that I would have to spend the day smiling and shaking hands and pretending that everything was going according to plan."[13]

In March 2000, Rush easily defeated Obama in the primary and then won reelection to Congress. Later, Obama realized he probably should not have challenged Rush. Even after he was elected to the U.S. Senate in 2004, Obama said he still felt the sting of that loss. For a time, he thought about leaving politics altogether. But instead, he told himself he would work harder and win more political friends to advance his career.

When the campaign ended, Obama returned to his old jobs of teaching and working in the Illinois Senate. He had given up his job at the law firm before starting his race for the House of Representatives. The next year, on June 10, 2001, the Obama family grew with the birth of a second daughter, Sasha. Once again, Obama tried to juggle the demands of being a father with a newborn and a busy career. The family had some trouble with money, as Obama had used some of his own funds for his 2000 campaign. He and Michelle were also still paying off loans that they had taken to pay for law school. At one point, he could not rent a car while traveling. He had no credit left on his credit card. He rarely spent money on himself, refusing to buy new clothes. In 2002, Michelle got a new job with the University of Chicago Hospital, which helped increase the family's finances.

FOCUS ON TERRORISM AND WAR

That year, world attention was focusing on Iraq. U.S. president George Bush was considering going to war with that country. He told Americans that Iraqi leader Saddam Hussein had **weapons of mass destruction (WMD)** and ties to terrorists. The world had seen the dangers of terrorism on September 11, 2001, with the al Qaeda attacks on the United States. Bush was seeking support from other countries and U.S. lawmakers for this possible war with Iraq.

"I don't oppose all wars....What I am opposed to is a dumb war."
—Barack Obama

In October 2002, a crowd gathered at a rally in Chicago to protest the possible war. Obama spoke, telling the crowd, "I don't oppose all wars....What I am opposed to is a dumb war."[14] Obama believed Iraq posed no threat to the United States, and Americans had other problems—such as fighting al Qaeda in Afghanistan. The speech did not draw much attention at the time. But the following year, the United States, the United Kingdom, and other nations did invade Iraq. In the years that followed, the war dragged on and became unpopular in the United States, United Kingdom, and other countries that originally supported the war. The world also learned that Iraq did not have WMDs, as President Bush had claimed. Obama reminded people that he had long opposed the Iraq War.

Shortly after that speech, in the fall election, the Democrats took control of the Illinois Senate. With his party in control, Obama could pass more of the laws he sponsored. But even before the November 2002 election, Obama was thinking about the future. He wanted to run for the U.S. Senate.

Terrorist Attack Kills Almost 3,000

New York City – September 11, 2001

On the morning of September 11, airplanes crashed into each of the so-called Twin Towers at the World Trade Center, killing nearly three thousand people, including about 500 people from other countries. The buildings collapsed soon after the attack. At almost the same time, another plane was flown into the Pentagon. This building, just outside Washington D.C., is the office of the U.S. Department of Defense, which runs the country's military. A fourth plane crashed in a field in Pennsylvania. All four planes were taken over by terrorists believed to be connected to a group called al Qaeda. Its leader, Osama bin Laden, was thought to be living in Afghanistan. Al Qaeda had carried out earlier attacks on U.S. targets around the world. President George W. Bush told Americans, "These acts of mass murder were intended to frighten our nation into chaos and retreat. But they have failed; our country is strong....None of us will ever forget this day. Yet, we go forward to defend freedom and all that is good and just in our world."[15]

Smoke is seen pouring out of the Twin Towers. Both buildings collapsed shortly after, leaving a gaping hole in Lower Manhattan.

65

One aide tried to convince Obama not to run. Campaigning for a national office requires a lot of time and travel. Obama had been away from his family often during his 2000 race against Bobby Rush. Michelle was not happy about all the time she and the girls were alone. The aide warned Obama that a Senate race could damage his relationship with his wife. Obama understood those concerns. But he wanted to do more to serve the public and make positive changes. He told the aide, "I'm not going to be able to help people if I'm stuck in the state senate for 20 years."[16]

The U.S. senator up for reelection in 2004 was Peter Fitzgerald, a Republican. Obama saw he was not widely popular and could be ripe for defeat.[17] Obama quietly began to look for people who would back his campaign. Some said they would support him, but they thought he had little chance of winning. Few people around Illinois knew Obama. He would have less money to spend than other candidates in the Democratic primary. Obama and his aides began calling possible donors to ask for money. Sometimes people hung up on them. Often, they would not return calls. Obama later wrote, "It was not fun."[18] But Obama kept working, hoping to make it to Washington D.C. ❖

Rise of the "Blogosphere"

As Barack Obama was starting his race for the Senate, a new technology was about to change U.S. politics. Across the world, more Internet users were posting their thoughts and linking to other websites using blogs. The word comes from "web logs," which people created as personal online journals. Some technology experts began to talk about the "blogosphere"—the total of all the blogs available, and the way they often linked together. Politicians and their supporters soon began starting blogs to discuss their views on different issues. Politicians also started websites where they sought donations. This technology helped spread information about Obama when he ran for president. The blogosphere sometimes contains rumors. But bloggers also provide links to sites with accurate facts.

HEADLINES FROM OBAMA'S FIRST YEARS IN THE U.S. SENATE

Here are some major news stories from the time.

Money Approved to Fight AIDS in Africa

Washington, D.C. – January 23, 2004

President George W. Bush signed into a law a bill that provides new money to fight the AIDS epidemic in Africa. The funds are part of a five-year program the president first announced in 2003 to help stop the spread of that deadly disease. AIDS—acquired immune deficiency syndrome—is caused by the human immunodeficiency virus (HIV) and weakens the body's ability to fight off diseases. There is no cure for AIDS, but certain medicines can slow its development. During the 1990s, the disease spread quickly through large parts of Africa, and about 70 percent of all AIDS patients in the world live there. The money from the United States will help buy drugs for people with AIDS and educate others about how to prevent its spread.

Earthquake, Powerful Tsunami Strike South Asia, Killing Tens of Thousands

December 26, 2004

Condoleezza Rice Becomes First Female African American to Serve as U.S. Secretary of State

January 26, 2005

People are rescued from ther rooftops after Hurricane Katrina hit. Most of the city is completely under water.

Flood Waters Rise After Hurricane Katrina

New Orleans, Louisiana August 29–30, 2005

A **levee** holding back Lake Pontchartrain gave way today, releasing more water into this city already damaged by Hurricane Katrina. The powerful storm, with winds over 225 km/hr (140 miles per hour) struck the Gulf Coast yesterday, destroying property in Mississippi, Alabama, and Louisiana. In New Orleans, about 80 percent of the city is under water. Tens of thousands of people who fled their homes are now stranded in two major city buildings, the Superdome and the Convention Center. So far, the U.S. government has not sent aid, such as food, water or medicine.

United Nations to Send Peacekeepers to Darfur Region of Sudan; Violence There Has Killed More Than 200,000 Since 2003

August 31, 2006

Senator Obama

Before he officially sought a seat in the U.S. Senate, Barack Obama had to win the support of one important person: his wife Michelle. The race for the Senate would be much longer than any campaign Obama had been in before. If he were elected, he would have even less time to spend with his family. Michelle agreed he should run, but as Obama wrote in The Audacity of Hope, *she joked that, "given the orderly life she preferred for our family, I shouldn't necessarily count on her vote."[1]*

Obama also had the support of Emil Jones. The president of the senate let Obama sponsor hundreds of bills, so he could try to win votes from the people who benefitted from the new laws. Slowly, Obama became better known, but as 2004 began, he was facing a tough fight in the Democratic primary. One of his opponents, Dan Hynes, was the son of an important politician in Chicago. People knew his name, and he had help from his father's friends. The other major rival was Blair Hull, a multi-millionaire. He used his own money to tell voters about his campaign.

RACE FOR THE SENATE

As the race began, Obama traveled across Illinois, sometimes with aides or friends, sometimes by himself. He spoke to small groups of people in private homes and visited churches, factories, and clubs. He later wrote,

> *"I think people are more concerned about a candidate's message than his color."*
> —Barack Obama

"Sometimes, after several hours of driving, I would find just two or three people waiting for me around a kitchen table."[2] But the visits gave Obama the chance to talk to people—and to listen to their concerns. They worried about having decent jobs, giving their children good educations, being protected from crime. And though they didn't want the government to solve all their problems, "they figured that government should help."[3] Obama knew if he won the election, he could try to bring that help. He used the slogan "Yes We Can" to inspire voters' hope for the future.

As the campaign went on, Obama had luck on his side. Peter Fitzgerald had decided not to run again for his Senate seat. The Republicans would have to hold their own primary, and the candidates would have to spend time and money on that race. Obama also won favorable reports from the media. Some reporters were interested in him because he was an **underdog** with an unusual background.[4] But at times, he still faced suspicion from some African Americans that he was not enough like them. Michelle helped him win some support from important blacks in Chicago. Obama also stressed laws he passed in the Illinois senate that helped African Americans. Several of these laws tried to make sure police officers fairly treated blacks suspected of committing crimes.

Obama's biggest break came in February 2004, just a few weeks before the primary. According to opinion polls, Blair Hull was in the lead. But reports spread about some personal problems he had with his former wife, and he lost support. Meanwhile, Obama had won the backing of several well-known U.S. senators, including Hillary Clinton. She was one of the best-known political leaders in the country. Her husband Bill had served as U.S. president from 1993 to 2001. In 2001, Hillary became the first former First Lady (president's wife) to serve in the Senate.

When the primary came, Obama won easily. He did well with white voters across Illinois, as well as with blacks in the cities. He said, "I think people are more concerned about a candidate's message than his color."[5] The win brought him some national attention. At the time, no African Americans served in the U.S. Senate. Only two had served during the past 100 years. Obama would become a national leader of African Americans—if he could win the election in the fall. But Obama did not want to be seen as just representing black Americans. "I'm rooted in the African American community, but I'm not limited by it."[6] He believed the issues he supported concerned all Americans.

Obama on the Issues

As a politician, Barack Obama has always worked to help strengthen the rights of African Americans and protect the interests of the poor and middle class. But he has supported other issues as well. During the 2004 Senate race, he mentioned some of his concerns:

• Ending the war in Iraq

• Improving transportation, through new airports and railroad lines

• Providing better and cheaper health care to all Americans

• Ending tax cuts for companies that close U.S. plants and send jobs overseas

• Preventing citizens from buying high-powered assault rifles

Obama's next opponent was Republican Jack Ryan. Like Obama, he was young, smart and a graduate of Harvard Law. Like Blair Hull, he was a millionaire with plenty of his own money to spend. But also like Hull, Ryan had problems with his former wife. When the media reported this, Ryan began to lose support. By the end of June, he decided to drop out of the race.

HIS FIRST MAJOR SPEECH

Obama kept campaigning as he waited for the Republicans to choose someone to take Ryan's spot. He also prepared for his first major speech in front of a national audience. Senator John Kerry was the Democratic candidate for president that year. He asked Obama to speak at the party's national convention in July. Kerry and Obama had appeared together in Illinois a few times. Obama impressed Kerry with his ability to connect with voters. Kerry said Obama "should be one of the faces of our party now, not years from now."[7]

Senate candidate Barack Obama delivers the keynote speech at the Democratic National Convention on July 27, 2004.

Squeezing in time to write whenever he could, Obama spent about 20 hours writing his speech. For several weeks, he worked at night in hotel rooms or in "the Hole," a small room off the family's kitchen at their Hyde Park home. Obama always enjoyed his late-night time alone, when he could relax, read, or answer emails.

A Handy Device

While campaigning and in Washington, Barack Obama relied on his personal digital assistant (PDA) to stay in touch with friends and aides. The device combines a wireless phone with a Web browser. With PDAs, users can send email or explore the Internet almost anywhere they travel. The type Obama used was introduced in 2002. After Obama's election as president in 2008, government officials told him he could no longer use his PDA. They could not guarantee that other people would not be able to read his email. As president, Obama would often receive secret information, and he could not risk others seeing it. But in January 2009, he received a new PDA with special security features that make it harder for anyone to secretly view his messages.

Writing the new speech was not hard. "It came out fairly fast," he told one reporter. "I had been thinking about these things for two years at that point."[8] He produced a speech that said all Americans are more alike than they are different. In the speech he said, "There's not a liberal America and a conservative America; there's the United States of America. There's not a black America and white America and Latino America and Asian America; there's the United States of America." After giving the speech in Boston on July 27, Obama was the country's newest political star. Chicago mayor Richard Daley said, "He had passion and emotion. And that's what it's all about."[9] He and other Illinois Democrats were sure Obama would win his race for the U.S. Senate.

ELECTION VICTORY

But the campaign was not over, and at times it was tiring. During the summer, Obama traveled with his family, but he rarely saw his daughters. During the day, aides took them to amusement parks while he and Michelle campaigned. By the time Obama got back to the hotel at night, Malia and Sasha were in bed. And as he traveled, the crowds coming to see him grew. He had less time to talk to people directly or sign autographs, as he had in the past.

November 2, 2004: Barack and Michelle Obama hold their daughters Malia and Sasha as they celebrate Mr. Obama's election to the U.S. senate. Obama defeated Republican candidate Alan Keyes to win the seat.

The Republicans soon picked Alan Keyes as a replacement for Jack Ryan. Like Obama, Keyes was a well-educated African American. But he had never lived in Illinois and had little campaign money to spend. And unlike Obama, he was very conservative and often said things that offended people. During the race, Keyes questioned if Obama were a true Christian. Keyes said Obama had voted to protect the legal right of women to have abortions, which many Christians opposed. Obama was always known for being able to control his emotions, no matter what. Keyes, he later wrote, got "under my skin in a way that few people ever have."[10] But with his huge lead in the polls, Obama did not have to worry much about Keyes. On Election Day, 70 percent of Illinois voters chose the 43-year-old Obama as their next U.S. senator.

Obama and his wife decided that the family would stay in Chicago while he worked in Washington. This meant the new senator would have to travel back and forth between the two cities. To help Obama stay in touch, Michelle bought him and the girls webcams. With them, they could see each other as they talked on the phone.

Obama fell into a set routine. In Washington, he spent long hours working. He proposed new laws and studied bills other lawmakers wrote. He gave speeches, met with Illinois voters visiting the capital, and went to meetings. Every Thursday morning, he visited with Illinoisans who came to Washington D.C. Sometimes he autographed books for children who came, writing, "Dream big dreams."[11] In Obama's spare time, he worked out in a gym, jogged, or spent time with friends, sometimes enjoying a steak dinner.

"Dream big dreams."
—Barack Obama

Here Senator Barack Obama arrives for President George W. Bush's State of the Union address to Congress.

WORKING IN THE SENATE

As a new senator, Obama needed to make connections with other lawmakers, both Republicans and Democrats. He joined with Republicans to sponsor some bills, including one to stop the spread of nuclear weapons. On a trip to Ukraine and Russia, he watched workers destroy old weapons, so terrorists would not be able to use them.

Obama's workweek usually ended on Thursday afternoons. He flew back to Chicago, where he and his family had a new home. With his election to the Senate, he received a contract to write a second book. His publisher also released new copies of *Dreams from My Father*, and they sold well. With the money from the books, the Obamas paid off their old debts and bought a large house in Hyde Park.

On his trips home, Obama spent as much time with Malia and Sasha as he could. He took them to school, went to their dance recitals and soccer games, and helped arrange their birthday parties. At night, the girls and their parents sometimes played Scrabble and other board games. Still, at times work forced him to miss family events or delay taking a vacation. Obama wrote, "I may tell myself that in some larger sense I am in politics for Malia and Sasha, that the work I do will make the world a better place for them."[12]

The visits back to Illinois were not just for the family. Through 2005, Obama held 39 town-hall meetings. In these meetings, he visited small towns and large cities, asking voters to come and discuss their concerns. He also traveled abroad. Along with his trip to Russia and Ukraine, he visited Israel and Iraq. Being a senator, Obama learned, required a lot of travel and time with the public. His aides carefully managed what he said and did. Reporters would print anything he said in public, and the aides wanted to be sure he did not offend his supporters. One aide said to a reporter, "The Barack you knew in the campaign…he's gone now….He doesn't have time to be himself except when he is with Michelle."[13]

Obama limited his time with the national TV networks and newspapers. He wanted to show that he was interested in working hard and not just winning attention.[14] Still, he and his aides knew many reporters carefully followed his actions. Some people already wondered if he was considering running for president. Obama always said no. But his aides knew he could perhaps be a candidate for vice president in 2008. And some even privately thought he could run for president that year.

IN THE PUBLIC EYE

In 2005, at 44 years old, Obama won national attention when he spoke out about Hurricane Katrina. In New Orleans, Louisiana, the storm had left tens of thousands of poor people homeless. Most of them were black. Some African Americans blamed racism for the government's slow

August 26, 2006: Barack Obama walks with his arm around his grandmother, Sarah Hussein Onyango Obama, during his visit to the Kenyan village Nyangoma-Kogelo.

reaction to their troubles. Obama, however, did not. He said the problem was a more general lack of concern with poverty in many U.S. cities. The struggles to find good jobs and housing affected many Americans, not just blacks. But he admitted the problems of the inner city tended to hit African Americans hardest.

The next year, Obama made a trip to Africa. He went partly to talk about issues, such as the spread of AIDS. He and Michelle each went to get a blood test in Kisumu, Kenya, to show Africans how easy it was to learn if they had the disease. In some African nations, leaders and citizens still did not understand everything about the disease. They did not know how deadly it was or take steps to stop its spread. Obama hoped his taking the AIDS test would convince Africans they could do more to fight the disease.

Obama also took time in Kenya to visit some of his relatives. Across the country, he was welcomed as a hero. He spoke out against the killings in Darfur, a part of Sudan. In South Africa, he visited the prison cell where Nelson Mandela had lived for many years. Mandela had been arrested for protesting South Africa's racist system. That system finally ended in 1992, and he was later elected the country's first black president.

The Africa trip brought Obama more national attention. So did the release of *The Audacity of Hope*. That fall, he made his first appearance on the cover of *Time*. The news magazine is read by millions of people around the world every week. Obama's fame had kept building since his 2004 speech at the Democratic National Convention. As 2006 came to an end, Obama wrestled with a tough decision: Should he run for president in 2008? Some people argued he did not have the experience to be president. But several friends thought he should run while he was so famous and well liked. One Illinois lawmaker said, "Barack's in a category of his own right now….I think 2008 is just the right time."[15]

That December, Obama took his family to Hawaii, as he did each year. He and Michelle discussed how a campaign for president would change their lives. Obama would have even less time for his family, less time for himself. Michelle said he should run, but on one condition. He had to give up cigarettes, which he had smoked since he was a teen. Obama agreed. Then, in the weeks to come, he prepared to tell the world he wanted to be president of the United States. ❖

European Nations Criticize U.S. on Guantánamo

Strasbourg, France – April 26, 2005

The Council of Europe condemned treatment of prisoners held at the U.S. naval base in Guantánamo Bay, Cuba. The United States began holding suspected terrorists there shortly after the September 11, 2001, al Qaeda attacks. Most of the several hundred prisoners at the base were captured during fighting in Afghanistan. The U.S. government has refused to charge the suspected terrorists with any specific crimes and has denied them legal rights normally given to prisoners of war or people arrested in the United States. The Parliamentary Assembly of the Council of Europe found that "many if not all **detainees** have been subjected to cruel, inhuman or degrading treatment occurring as a direct result of official policy..."[16] The assembly called for the United States to take several steps, including "to allow all detainees to challenge the lawfulness of their detention before a regularly constituted court... [and] to release immediately all those detainees against whom there is not sufficient evidence to justify laying criminal charges."[17]

Headlines from Obama's Time as a Presidential Candidate

Here are some major news stories from the time.

International Group Releases New Warnings of Dangers of Global Warming; Human Activity Likely to Blame

February 2, 2007

Bush's Approval Rating Hits New Low

New York – November 3, 2008

A new poll shows that just 20 percent of Americans approve of George W. Bush, his lowest level of support during his presidency. The unpopular war in Iraq and current economic troubles have hurt the president's popularity. The new numbers come just one day before the election to choose the next president of the United States. Since his reelection in 2005, Bush has been a "lame duck," meaning he could not run again and so had less influence. Other politicians are less likely to work with a lame duck, since they know that person will not be in power long. Bush's low poll numbers have led even some members of his own party to limit their contact with him during the 2008 campaign.[1]

Terrorists Attack Mumbai Hotels, Killing Dozens; Possible Connection to Pakistan

November 26, 2008

Buenos Aires, Argentina: A trader in the Buenos Aires Stock Exchange deals with the worsening outlook of the global financial system. With the U.S. entering recession, Latin American stock markets plunged sharply, along with other stock markets around the world.

Financial Crisis Hits U.S., Sparks Recession Worldwide

Cambridge, Massachusetts – December 1, 2008

The National Bureau of Economic Research (NBER) confirmed what many Americans have long believed: The United States economy has been weakening throughout 2008. A recession is a decline in economic activity, with consumers buying fewer goods and companies firing workers. During 2008, the U.S. stock market fell sharply after several major banks failed or came close to failure. This decline came after a crisis in the housing market. A growing number of people could not make payments on loans they previously took to buy homes. As they stopped paying, the homeowners sometimes had to sell their homes for less than they were worth or turn them over to the banks. The recession goes beyond the United States. Japan also just announced it was in recession, and some European countries face recession as well.

Oil Prices Fall to Lowest Level in Four Years; Drop More than $100 per Barrel Since Record Prices Set in July

December 5, 2008

Making History

On a cold February day in 2007, Barack Obama stood outside the Old State Capitol in Springfield, Illinois. About 17,000 people had gathered to hear his first official speech as a candidate for president.

COMPARED TO LINCOLN

Some reporters noted that President Abraham Lincoln had started his rise to fame inside the old capitol. Like Obama, he had once been an Illinois lawmaker. Other people saw more traits the two men shared. Both were tall. Both were lawyers. Both spoke and wrote well. And Lincoln was linked to an important part of African American history. He had freed most U.S. slaves during the Civil War. As early as 2004, one Chicago reporter said Obama could be "the most significant political figure Illinois has sent to Washington since Abraham Lincoln."[1]

Obama had long respected Lincoln and his efforts to keep the North and South together in 1861. He knew the role Lincoln played in helping blacks gain their freedom. He also admired the way Lincoln combined the desire to do what was practical with what he thought was right.

Obama mentioned Lincoln often in his speech that day at the state house. Lincoln tells us, Obama said, "that beneath all the differences of race and region, faith and station, we are one people. He tells us that there is power in hope."[2] Obama also spoke about the issues that were important to him. He wanted to hire more teachers and improve education. He wanted to improve medical care for the poor. He thought the United

> *"Together, starting today, let us finish the work that needs to be done, and usher in a new birth of freedom on this Earth."*
> —Barack Obama

States should look for new energy sources and stop using oil bought overseas. He blamed past leaders for not taking bold steps to solve the country's problems. Finally, Obama said, "I'm ready to take up the cause, and march with you, and work with you. Together, starting today, let us finish the work that needs to be done, and usher in a new birth of freedom on this Earth."[3]

With the speech over, the hard work began. Obama traveled across the country to win support and money. He was competing against seven other people for the Democratic nomination. Senator Hillary Clinton and former senator John Edwards were the best known of them. Edwards had run for vice president in 2004.

As the 2008 campaign progressed, the competition between Barack Obama and Hillary Clinton became increasingly intense. Their race to win the Democratic Party's nomination was historic in its own right. It was also, in many ways, more hard-fought than the following general election.

Another Harvard Product

Social networking sites such as Facebook let friends link to each other and keep track of what they're doing. After Barack Obama started his own Facebook page in 2007, thousands of people soon linked to him. Facebook was created in 2004 by Mark Zuckerberg. At the time, he was a student at Harvard. He created the site so other students could easily keep in contact with each other. From Harvard, Facebook spread to high schools and other colleges, and soon anyone could use it. Obama's aides still maintain his Facebook site to keep voters informed of his plans.

Obama started out strong, collecting almost $25 million in donations in just a few months. A lot of this money came from donations made on the Internet. Obama appealed to many young voters who visited the website Facebook or wrote blogs. Facebook is a social network site, where people can keep in contact with friends and make new ones online. Some of these young supporters volunteered to help the campaign. Obama also hired experienced aides to run his campaign.

"In every audience I have seen, there is a jolt of pure electric energy at those closing words. Tears stain some cheeks—and some people look a little thunderstruck."

—A reporter

When Obama began debating the other candidates in public, he didn't always speak as well as he could. He seemed to lack energy or had trouble coming up with good answers. He watched one tape of himself debating and said, "It's worse than I thought."[4] Obama now counted on the skills he had learned as a community organizer to help him win votes. He talked to as many people as possible and earned their trust. Then he asked them to take action to help him. Once again, he used the slogan, "Yes We Can."

By November of 2007, he had perfected a campaign speech. It made the crowds he spoke to stand and cheer. He ended the speech by saying, "Let's go change the world." A reporter who often watched these speeches wrote, "In every audience I have seen, there is a jolt of pure electric energy at those closing words. Tears stain some cheeks—and some people look a little thunderstruck."[5]

WINNING THE CAUCUSES

In 2008, the Democratic candidates faced each other in a series of primaries and special meetings called caucuses. Democrats in each state voted for the candidate they wanted to be the nominee for president. Each state would send a certain number of people called delegates to the national convention in August. The delegates would vote for the candidate the voters of their state had favored in the primaries and caucuses.

The first caucus was held in January in Iowa. Hillary Clinton and her aides thought she would win. They were stunned when Obama beat her.[6] Clinton won the next vote, in New Hampshire. As other candidates dropped out, Obama and Clinton fought for the nomination. The winner would make history, since neither a woman nor a black man had ever run for president from a major political party.

After New Hampshire, Obama won several more states and began to increase his lead over Clinton. She began to run ads that suggested

Obama did not have the experience to be president. In March, she won the delegates from several large states. But Obama was winning more often and kept the lead. Trouble came, though, when the media released comments made by Obama's old friend and minister, Jeremiah Wright.

FACING CONTROVERSIES

In his church, Wright had often spoken strongly against racism. The media published some of his remarks, such as "Racism is how this country was founded and how this country is still run!"[7] Some people wondered if Obama agreed with some of Wright's more extreme comments about racism in America. Obama said he did not. "I had not heard him make such…objectionable remarks…had I heard him while I was in church, I would have objected."[8] The Wright incident began a pattern that lasted throughout the campaign. People who opposed Obama suggested his views were too extreme for him to be president.

Obama had long called himself African American, even though he came from a mixed racial background. As the questions about Wright arose, Obama decided to speak about race in the United States. He talked about his white mother and grandparents. He mentioned that even Toot, his grandmother, sometimes held racist views. And he knew Reverend Wright said some things about whites that were unfair. Wright had focused on "what is wrong with America above all that we know is right with America."[9] But Obama admitted some African Americans were still angry over how they were badly treated in the past, and sometimes still today. He knew more work had to be done to unite people of all backgrounds. Obama finished his speech by talking about a young white woman and an old black man who both supported him. Obama saw that his campaign could be a step toward bringing more blacks and whites together. He sometimes mentioned his mixed racial roots as a way to explain what is best about America. People from different backgrounds work together to make the country strong.

After the incident with Wright, Obama also faced attacks because of his past political friendships. A Chicago business owner named Tony Rezko had often given money to his campaigns. Obama had also bought property from Rezko that sat next to the Obamas' expensive Chicago home. In 2008, Rezko was on trial for corruption. The media began to report on Obama's friendship with Rezko. Obama said he had not seen him recently. He also figured out how much money Rezko had given him over the years and donated the same amount to charity. Still, critics wondered if Obama had ever done something illegal while involved in Chicago politics.

Despite these problems, Obama continued to win delegates and by June he had enough for the nomination. He had started the campaign as an underdog to Hillary Clinton. She was better known and had the support of many important Democrats. But Obama had caught the attention of many voters with his promise for change. He also supported issues that concerned many people. As before, he talked about giving more Americans health care they could afford. He wanted to spend more money on education. He thought Congress should raise taxes on wealthier Americans to pay for some of his programs. And in foreign affairs, he wanted to take U.S. troops out of Iraq and send more to Afghanistan.

A LONG CAMPAIGN

Obama's win over Clinton did not give him time to rest. Now he had to focus on defeating Senator John McCain, the Republican candidate.

"If I ever thought this [running for president] was ruining my family, I wouldn't do it."
—Barack Obama

The long, tiring, campaign made it almost impossible for Obama to do the things he usually did as a father. He rarely had time for his daughters' piano recitals or meeting with their teachers. He also missed the mornings in bed when the girls would come in to greet Michelle and him. But whenever he could, he read books to them—even when his throat was sore from talking to so many people every day. As he told one reporter, "If I ever thought this [running for president] was ruining my family, I wouldn't do it."[10]

Through the summer, Obama continued to make speeches and talk with the media. He told one magazine some of the music he kept on his iPod: songwriter Bob Dylan, jazz trumpeter Miles Davis, hip-hop star Jay Z.

October 7, 2008: Barack Obama speaks to the audience at Belmont University's Nashville, Tennessee campus. John McCain listens to his opponent during the second debate of the 2008 presidential campaign.

He also talked about more serious issues, saying, "I want people to feel connected to their government again, and I want that government to respond to the voices of the people…"[11]

In August, the Obamas traveled to Denver, Colorado, for the Democratic National Convention. On August 28, Obama spoke in front of 84,000 people in Denver's football stadium. Television networks also delivered the speech to millions of homes. He said President Bush's actions in Iraq and elsewhere had hurt the United States. John McCain would mostly follow Bush's policies. If Americans wanted change, they needed to vote for him. He said, "Change happens because the American people demand it—because they rise up and insist on new ideas and new leadership, a new politics for a new time. America, this is one of those moments."[12]

In his speeches, John McCain said that Obama lacked the experience to be president during such tough times. The United States was fighting wars in Iraq and Afghanistan. It still faced the danger of new terrorist attacks. McCain had served in the military. He had been in Congress for more than 20 years. He told voters that he, not Obama should lead the country during difficult times.

"Change happens because the American people demand it—because they rise up and insist on new ideas and new leadership, a new politics for a new time. America, this is one of those moments."
—Barack Obama

Through the fall, polls showed that Obama held a small lead over McCain. The candidates met in several debates, and Obama remained on top. The economy worsened through that time, and Obama said McCain did not truly understand the problems Americans faced. He, not McCain, would be able to fix the economy and make sure people had jobs.

Despite his lead, Obama faced some tough moments. He faced questions about another past relationship. In Chicago, he had worked with and lived near William Ayers. During the early 1970s, Ayers belonged to a group that opposed the Vietnam War. It bombed several buildings to try to force the United States to end the war. During the 2008 campaign, some Americans worried that Obama might support radical ideas, since he had been friendly with Ayers. Obama said he and Ayers had not been very close, and he opposed the violent actions Ayers and his group once used. Despite the questions, Obama kept his lead in the polls.

On November 3, the day before Election Day, Obama campaigned in Florida and North Carolina. In between speeches, he learned that his grandmother Toot had died in Hawaii. She had been sick for some time, and Obama had briefly left his campaign to see her. He was glad he had made that last visit, after not seeing his mother just before her death. In North Carolina, Obama told the crowd about his grandmother, calling her a "quiet hero."[13] Then he did something he rarely did in public—he cried.

ELECTION DAY

On Election Day, Obama went home to Chicago to vote, then met with voters in Indiana. That evening, in downtown Chicago, several hundred thousand people began to gather in Grant Park. Obama planned to speak there after the voting ended. His supporters hoped they would be celebrating an Obama win.

"...a man who can get some things done, at a time when so many of their leaders...cannot."
—*Time* magazine

Obama was calm as the results began to come in, even as the voting ended in California, he realized he would be the first African American president of the United States. In his speech in Grant Park, Obama once again mentioned Abraham Lincoln. He thanked everyone who had helped him win. And he said the future would not be easy, "so let us summon a new spirit of patriotism…where each of us resolves to pitch in and work harder and look after not only ourselves, but each other."[14]

Many people in the park and watching on TV cried with joy as they heard Obama speak. They had never thought America could overcome racism and elect a black president. They were also inspired by Obama's

The Obama family walks out to greet the huge crowd gathered for Obama's election night rally in Chicago's Grant Park.

promise to make the country better. The good feelings went beyond the United States. People celebrated in Kenya and other countries, and many world leaders welcomed Obama's victory.

Obama had to wait more than two months before his **inauguration**. During that time, the economy was continuing to decline, and that became his major concern. Obama chose advisors who would help him deal with this and other problems when he took office. The media also continued to assess the importance of Obama and his victory. Through 2008, *Time* had featured him on its cover 14 times. In December, the magazine named Obama its "Person of the Year," saying it was hard to believe "that half the people in America had never heard of him two years ago." Now, *Time* reported, some voters saw him as "a man who can get some things done, at a time when so many of their leaders... cannot."[15]

"...the challenges we face are real, they are serious and they are many. They will not be met easily or in a short span of time. But know this America: They will be met."
—Barack Obama

Finally, Inauguration Day arrived. Writers and reporters from the Internet, newspapers, and other media noted the importance of the day. On January 20, 2009, Obama became the first African American president of the United States. In his first speech, Obama did not talk about this great achievement. Instead, he admitted he and the nation faced a crisis. The United States was still at war in Iraq and Afghanistan, the economy had continued to decline, and health care cost too much. Yet Obama also offered hope. He said, "the challenges we face are real, they are serious and they are many. They will not be met easily or in a short span of time. But know this America: They will be met."[16] He then outlined what he planned to do: create new jobs, build new roads, reduce the use of oil to create energy, lower the cost of medical care. The country would face new challenges, Obama said, but it had the tools to meet them: "honesty and hard work, courage and fair play, tolerance and curiosity, loyalty and patriotism."[17] Americans had to realize "that we have duties to ourselves, our nation, and the world."

Perhaps the most urgent problem Obama faced was the U.S. economy, which was suffering in the worldwide recession. He signed measures to increase government spending, to support financial institutions, and to assist the car industry. Although unemployment continued to rise, these steps helped to restore confidence in the economy.

Overseas, Obama decided to reduce the number of U.S. soldiers in Iraq and, eventually, to end combat operations there. He ordered that the Guantanamo Bay camp holding terrorist suspects be closed by 2010. Later in 2009 he ordered that more troops should be sent to help win the war in Afghanistan. In a speech in Egypt he declared: "I've come here to Cairo to seek a new beginning between the United States and Muslims around the world, one based on mutual interest and mutual respect..." [18] He also had to respond to two unexpected developments: security failures before an unsuccessful attack by a terrorist trying to blow up an airliner on Christmas Day 2009, and the appalling devastation caused by the Haiti earthquake in January 2010.

To many people's surprise, Obama was awarded the 2009 Nobel Peace Prize for his "extraordinary efforts to strengthen international diplomacy and cooperation between peoples" and for his work for a world free of nuclear weapons.[19] President Obama had already made a huge impact on the world. ❖

Timeline

1961   Barack Obama is born to Barack Obama Senior and Ann Dunham Obama in Honolulu, Hawaii, on August 4

1963   MARTIN LUTHER KING JR. DELIVERS HIS "I HAVE A DREAM" SPEECH IN WASHINGTON D.C.

PRESIDENT JOHN F. KENNEDY IS KILLED IN DALLAS, TEXAS

1964   Obama's parents divorce

1965   THE CIVIL RIGHTS ACT OF 1965 ENSURES THE VOTING RIGHTS OF AFRICAN AMERICANS

1967   Obama and his mother move to Indonesia

1968   MARTIN LUTHER KING JR. IS KILLED IN MEMPHIS, TENNESSEE

1969   APOLLO 11 ASTRONAUTS ARE FIRST PEOPLE TO LAND ON THE MOON

1971   Obama returns to Hawaii and lives with his grandparents, Stanley and Madelyn Dunham

Obama sees his father for the last time

1974   PRESIDENT RICHARD NIXON RESIGNS

1975   U.S. TROOPS LEAVE SOUTH VIETNAM AND THE VIETNAM WAR ENDS

1977   THE TELEVISION MINISERIES ROOTS FIRST AIRS

1979   Obama graduates from high school

Obama goes to Occidental College in Los Angeles, California

MARGARET THATCHER IS ELECTED THE FIRST FEMALE PRIME MINISTER OF GREAT BRITAIN

1981   Obama transfers to Columbia University in New York

1982   Obama's father dies

1983   Obama graduates from Columbia

Obama begins working for Business International Corporation

TERRORISTS KILL 241 U.S. MARINES BASED IN BEIRUT, LEBANON

1985   Obama moves to Chicago to work as a community organizer

1987   THE UNITED STATES AND SOVIET UNION AGREE TO GET RID OF SOME OF THEIR NUCLEAR WEAPONS

1988   Obama visits relatives in Kenya for the first time

Obama enters law school at Harvard University

1989   Obama takes a summer job in Chicago and meets Michelle Robinson

THE BERLIN WALL OPENS

1990   Obama is elected as the *Harvard Law Review's* first African American president

1991   A **COALITION** OF THE UNITED STATES, GREAT BRITAIN, AND OTHER NATIONS UNITE TO DRIVE INVADING IRAQI TROOPS OUT OF KUWAIT DURING THE FIRST GULF WAR

Obama graduates from Harvard and returns to Chicago

1992   Obama runs Project Vote! and begins teaching at the University of Chicago

Michelle Robinson and Obama marry

1993   Obama begins working at a Chicago law firm

1994	NELSON MANDELA IS ELECTED THE FIRST BLACK PRESIDENT OF SOUTH AFRICA
1995	Obama publishes *Dreams from My Father*
	Ann Dunham dies of cancer
1996	Obama wins election to serve in the Illinois state senate
1998	Michelle and Barack Obama have their first child, a daughter named Malia
2000	Bobby Rush defeats Obama in the primary for Rush's seat in the U.S. House of Representatives
	HILLARY CLINTON WINS A U.S. SENATE SEAT FROM NEW YORK, BECOMING THE FIRST FORMER FIRST LADY TO HOLD A NATIONAL POLITICAL OFFICE
	THE U.S. SUPREME COURT RULES TO STOP RECOUNTING VOTES IN FLORIDA, GIVING GEORGE W. BUSH THE U.S. PRESIDENCY
2001	The Obamas have their second daughter, Sasha
	TERRORISTS TAKE CONTROL OF FOUR U.S. PLANES AND KILL ALMOST 3,000 PEOPLE
	U.S. AND BRITISH FORCES INVADE AFGHANISTAN, WHERE TERRORIST LEADER OSAMA BIN LADEN HAD BEEN LIVING
2002	Obama speaks out against a U.S. plan to invade Iraq
2003	INTERNATIONAL FORCES LED BY THE UNITED STATES INVADE IRAQ AND FORCE ITS LEADER, SADDAM HUSSEIN, FROM POWER
2004	Obama wins the Democratic nomination in Illinois to run for the U.S. Senate
	Obama speaks at the Democratic National Convention and becomes an instant political star
	Obama defeats Alan Keyes in their race for the U.S. Senate
	HUGE TSUNAMI KILLS HUNDREDS OF THOUSANDS OF PEOPLE IN SOUTH ASIA
2005	Obama begins traveling back and forth between his Senate job in Washington D.C. and his home in Chicago
	EUROPEAN NATIONS CONDEMN TREATMENT OF PRISONERS HELD BY THE UNITED STATES AT GUANTÁNAMO BAY, CUBA
	HURRICANE KATRINA DESTROYS LARGE PARTS OF NEW ORLEANS, LOUISIANA
2006	Obama visits Africa
	The Audacity of Hope, Obama's second book, is published
2007	NEW REPORT WARNS OF THE DANGERS OF GLOBAL WARMING
	Obama gives a speech in Springfield, Illinois announcing his candidacy for president
	Campaigns on Facebook and other Internet sites help Obama raise millions of dollars and recruit volunteers for his candidacy
2008	Obama wins the Iowa caucuses, the first election in the race for the Democratic nomination
	Obama defeats his main challenger, Hillary Clinton, to win the nomination
	Republicans raise questions about Obama's ties to corrupt people, radicals, and former U.S. terrorists
	MORE U.S. TROOPS GO TO AFGHANISTAN, WHERE INTERNATIONAL FORCES ARE STILL BATTLING TERRORISTS AND REBELS
	Obama defeats John McCain, becoming the first African American president of the United States
2009	Obama is sworn in as the 44th U.S. president on January 20

Glossary

apartheid legal system once used in South Africa to ensure whites controlled politics and the economy while denying rights to blacks and Asians

bill the basic outline of a new law, which must be approved by lawmakers and the president to take effect

campaign the process of running to win an election

coalition a group of countries or governments that form a temporary alliance with the purpose of accomplishing something

Communist relating to a political system in which the government owns all businesses, limits personal freedom, and prevents any challenges to its rule

conservative tending to think government should play a limited role in the economy and people's private lives; a person who supports that role

detainees people held by a government because they might have committed a crime

discrimination the act of denying someone their rights because of some personal trait, such as race or religion

economy the total goods and services produced in a particular region, such as a city or state

electoral votes the votes cast by representatives of the voters in each state to choose the U.S president

grassroots relating to small, local political organizations

inauguration the ceremony that officially gives a person a new title and powers, such as U.S. president

levee an earthen wall meant to hold back water

liberal tending to favor an active government role in the economy and other parts of life; a person who supports those actions

nomination the selection of a person to represent a particular party during an election

nuclear relating to the core, or nucleus of atoms, where tremendous amounts of energy are stored

primary an election held by a political party to choose its candidates

scholarship money given to a student to attend a school

Soviet Union former country consisting of Russia, Ukraine, and 13 other current Eastern European and Central Asian nations

stockyards places where animals are kept before they are killed and processed into meat

terrorist person who uses violence or fear to force others to do something

tolerant accepting of many different people or ideas

underdog person not favored to win an election or game

weapons of mass destruction (WMD) devices or substances that can kill thousands of people at once

Western relating to the United States, Great Britain, Canada, Australia, New Zealand, and European nations that have democratic governments

Notes on Sources

A KEYNOTE ADDRESS (PAGES 6–9)

1. Barack Obama, *The Audacity of Hope* (New York: Vintage Books, 2006), p. 424.
2. *Ibid.*
3. "Transcript: Illinois Senate Candidate Barack Obama." *Washington Post*, July 27. 2004. Available online. URL: http://www.washingtonpost.com/wp-dyn/articles/A19751-2004Jul27.html. Accessed November 7, 2008.
4. *Ibid.*
5. *Ibid.*
6. David Bernstein, "The Speech." *Chicago Magazine*, June 2007. Available online. URL: http://www.chicagomag.com/Chicago-Magazine/June-2007/The-Speech/. Accessed on November 6, 2008.
7. David Mendell, *Obama: From Promise to Power* (New York: Amistad, 2007), p. 285.
8. *Ibid.*
9. Randal C. Archibold, "Day After, Keynote Speaker Finds Admirers Everywhere." *New York Times*, July 29, 2004. Available online. URL: http://query.nytimes.com/gst/fullpage.html?res=9A03E7DB103DF93AA15754C0A9629C8B63. Accessed on November 7, 2008; Scott L. Malcomson, "An Appeal Beyond Race." *New York Times*, August 1, 2004. Available online. URL: http://query.nytimes.com/gst/fullpage.html?res=9406E7D71E3DF932A3575BC0A9629C8B63. Accessed on November 7, 2008.
10. Rick Pearson and David Mendell, "Democrats: We've Got a Winner in Obama." *Chicago Tribune*, July 29, 2004, p. 17.
11. Paul Steinhauser, "Poll: 76 Percent Say U.S. Ready for Black President." CNN, April 4, 2008. Available online. URL: http://www.cnn.com/2008/POLITICS/04/03/poll.black.president/index.html. Accessed on November 8, 2008.
12. "Barack Obama Speech." *Chicago Tribune*, November 4, 2008. Available online. URL: http://www.chicagotribune.com/news/politics/obama/chi-barack-obama-speech,0,524762.story?page=1. Accessed on November 7, 2008.

HEADLINES FROM OBAMA'S CHILDHOOD (PAGES 10–11)

1. Robert Torricelli and Andrew Carroll, eds. *In Their Own Words: Extraordinary Speeches of the American Century* (New York: Kodansha International, 1999), p.222.
2. Michael Nelson, ed. *The Presidency* (New York: Smithmark Publishers, 1996), pp. 157-161.
3. Torricelli and Carroll, *In Their Own Words*, p. 236.

OBAMA'S EARLY YEARS (PAGES 12–19)

1. Jennifer Steinhauer, "Charisma and a Search for Self in Obama's Hawaii Childhood." *New York Times*, March 17, 2007. Available online. URL: http://www.nytimes.com/2007/03/17/us/politics/17hawaii.html. Accessed on October 25, 2008.

2. Barack Obama, *Dreams from My Father* (New York: Three Rivers Press, 2004), p. 8.

3. *Ibid.*, pp. 22-23.

4. *Ibid.*, p. 30.

5. *Ibid.*, p. 37.

6. Obama, *Audacity of Hope*, p. 241.

7. Kirsten Scharnberg and Kim Barker, "The Not-So-Simple Story of Barack Obama's Youth." *Chicago Tribune*, March 25, 2007. Available online. URL: http://www.chicagotribune.com/news/politics/obama/chi-070325obama-youth-story-archive,0,3864722.story. Accessed November 2, 2008.

8. Obama, *Dreams from My Father*, pp. 47-48.

9. Amanda Ripley, "The Story of Barack Obama's Mother." *Time*, April 9, 2008. Available online. URL: http://www.time.com/time/nation/article/0,8599,1729524,00.html. Accessed on November 2, 2008.

10. Obama, *Dreams from My Father*, pp. 30, 51.

11. *Ibid.*, p. 52.

HEADLINES FROM OBAMA'S TEEN YEARS (PAGES 20–21)

1. Carroll Kilpatrick, "Nixon Resigns." *The Washington Post*, August 9, 1974. Available online. URL: http://www.washingtonpost.com/wp-srv/national/longterm/watergate/articles/080974-3.htm. Accessed on November 20, 2008.

2. Margaret Thatcher, "Remarks on Becoming Prime Minister." Margaret Thatcher Foundation, http://www.margaretthatcher.org/speeches/displaydocument.asp?docid=104078. Accessed on November 20, 2008.

EDUCATION OF A YOUNG MAN (PAGES 22–31)

1. Mendell, *Obama: From Promise to Power*, p. 36.

2. Obama, *Dreams from My Father*, p. 60.

3. "Tribal Bonds Color Kenyan Politics." CNN.com, January 2, 2008. http://www.cnn.com/2008/WORLD/africa/01/02/kenya.background/index.html. Accessed on January 8, 2009.

4. Obama, *Dreams from My Father*, pp. 69-70.

5. *Ibid.*, p. 63.

6. Steinhauer, "Charisma and a Search for Self in Obama's Hawaii Childhood."

7. Jaymes Song, "Obama Finds Refuge, Identity in Basketball." *USA Today*, June 16, 2008. Available online. URL: http://www.usatoday.com/news/politics/2008-06-16-4228899315_x.htm. Accessed on January 8, 2009; Mendell, *Obama: From Promise to Power*, p. 48.

8. Obama, *Dreams from My Father*, p. 94.

9. *Ibid.*, p. 82.

10. "1977 TV Series Changed How Americans View Race." Voice of America, January 30, 2002. Available online. URL: http://www.voanews.com/english/archive/2002-01/a-2002-01-30-41-1977.cfm. Accessed on November 21, 2008.

11. Obama, *Dreams from My Father*, p. 106.

12. *Ibid.*, p. 107.

13. *Ibid.*, p. 120

14. Maurice Possley, "Activism Blossomed in College." *Chicago Tribune*, March 30, 2007. Available online. URL: http://www.chicagotribune.com/news/nationworld/chi-0703291042mar30-archive,0,1533921.story. Accessed on November 22, 2008.

15. *Ibid.*, pp. 133-134.

16. Mendell, *Obama: From Promise to Power*, p. 62.

HEADLINES FROM OBAMA'S EARLY CHICAGO YEARS (PAGES 32–33)

1. Ronald Reagan, "Address to the Nation on the *Challenger* Disaster." January 28, 1986. Available online. URL: http://www.reaganfoundation.org/reagan/speeches/challenger.asp. Accessed on January 9. 2009.

IN THE COMMUNITY (PAGES 34–43)

1. Jessica Curry, "Barack Obama Under the Lights." *Chicago Life*, Fall 2004. Available online. URL: http://www.chicagolife.net/content/politics/Barack_Obama. Accessed on December 1, 2008.

2. Obama, *Dreams from My Father*, p. 142.

3. Bob Secter and John McCormick, "Barack Obama: Portrait of a Pragmatist." *Chicago Tribune*, March 30, 2007. Available online. URL: http://www.chicagotribune.com/news/nationworld/chi-0703300121mar30-archive,0,5213128.story. Accessed on November 26, 2008.

4. Obama, *Dreams from My Father*, p. 165.

5. Barack Obama. "Why Organize? Problems and Promise in the Inner City." *Illinois Issues*, University of Illinois at Springfield. Available online. URL: http://www.edwoj.com/Alinsky/AlinskyObamaChapter1990.htm. Accessed on December 1, 2008.

6. *Ibid.*

7. Secter and McCormick, "Barack Obama: Portrait of a Pragmatist."

8. Curry, "Barack Obama Under the Lights."

9. *Ibid.*

10. Secter and McCormick, "Barack Obama: Portrait of a Pragmatist."

11. Obama, *Dreams from My Father*, p. 221.

12. Mendell, *Obama: From Promise to Power*, p. 76.

13. Cathleen Falsani, "Obama: I Have a Deep Faith." *Chicago Sun-Times*, April 5, 2004. Available online. URL: http://www.suntimes.com/news/falsani/ 726619,obamafalsani040504.article. Accessed on December 1, 2008.

14. *Ibid.*; Obama. *Audacity of Hope*, p. 246;

15. Mendell, *Obama: From Promise to Power*, p. 82.

16. David Moberg. "Obama's Community Roots." *The Nation*, April 3, 2007. Available online. URL: http://www.thenation.com/doc/20070416/moberg. Accessed on December 1, 2008.

HEADLINES FROM OBAMA'S HARVARD YEARS AND RETURN TO CHICAGO (PAGES 44–45)

1. "1991: Jubilation Follows Gulf War Cease Fire." On This Day: February 28. BBC. Available online. URL: http://news.bbc.co.uk/onthisday/hi/dates/stories/february/28/ newsid_2515000/2515289.stm. Accessed on December 1, 2008.

HARVARD AND BACK (PAGES 46–55)

1. Obama, *Dreams from My Father*, p. 340.

2. Mendell, *Obama: From Promise to Power*, p. 86.

3. *Ibid.*, p. 87.

4. Liza Mundy, *Michelle* (New York: Simon & Schuster, 2008), p. 98.

5. Liza Mundy. "When Michelle Met Barack." *Washington Post*, October 5, 2008. Available online. URL: http://www.washingtonpost.com/wp-dyn/content/story/2008/10/03/ ST2008100302144.html. Accessed on November 6, 2008.

6. *Ibid.*

7. *Ibid.*

8. Tammerlin Drummond, "Barack Obama's Law Personality." *Los Angeles Times*. March 19, 1990. Available online. URL: http://latimesblogs.latimes.com/ thedailymirror/2008/09/barack-obama-ha.html. Accessed on December 2, 2008.

9. Mendell, *Obama: From Promise to Power*, p. 90.

10. Jodi Kantor, "In Law School, Obama Found Political Voice." *New York Times*, January 28, 2007. Available online. URL: http://www.nytimes.com/2007/01/28/us/politics/ 28obama.html. Accessed on December 2, 2008.

11. Drummond, "Barack Obama's Law Personality."

12. *Ibid.*

13. Mendell, *Obama: From Promise to Power*, p. 91.

14. "The Choice 2008." *Frontline*. Available online. URL: http://www.pbs.org/wgbh/ pages/frontline/choice2008/obama/harvard.html. Accessed December 3, 2008.

15. Gretchen Reynolds, "Vote of Confidence." *Chicago Magazine*, January 1993. Available online. URL: http://www.chicagomag.com/Chicago-Magazine/January-1993/Vote-of-Confidence. Accessed on December 3, 2008.

16. *Ibid.*

THE WORLD OF POLITICS (PAGES 58–67)

1. Obama, *Dreams from My Father*, p. *xii*.

2. Hank De Zutter, "What Makes Obama Run?" *Chicago Reader*, December 8, 1995. Available online. URL: http://www.chicagoreader.com/obama/951208/. Accessed on November 14, 2008.

3. Alexandra Starr, "Case Study." New York Times, September 21, 2008. Available online. URL: http://www.nytimes.com/2008/09/21/magazine/21obama-t.html/. Accessed on December 3. 2008.

4. Mendell, *Obama: From Promise to Power*, pp. 114-115, 121-122.

5. Obama, *The Audacity of Hope*, p. 62.

6. Mendell, *Obama: From Promise to Power*, p. 124.

7. Obama, *The Audacity of Hope*, p. 408.

8. Janny Scott, "In 2000, a Streetwise Veteran Schooled a Bold Young Obama." *New York Times*, September 9, 2007. Available online. URL: http://www.nytimes.com/2007/09/09/us/politics/09obama.html. Accessed on November 6, 2008.

9. Ted Kleine, "Is Bobby Rush in Trouble?" *Chicago Reader*, March 17, 2000. Available online. URL: http://www.chicagoreader.com/obama/000317/. Accessed December 5, 2008.

10. *Ibid.*

11. *Ibid.*

12. *Ibid.*

13. Obama, *The Audacity of Hope*, p. 127.

14. Don Gonyea, "Obama Still Stumps on 2002 Anti-War Declaration." National Public Radio, March 25, 2008. Available online. URL: http://www.npr.org/templates/story/story.php?storyId=88988093. Accessed on December 5, 2008.

15. "Statement by the President in His Address to the Nation." September 11, 2001. The White House. Available online. URL: http://www.whitehouse.gov/news/releases/2001/09/20010911-16.html. Accessed on December 4, 2008.

16. Liza Mundy, "A Series of Fortunate Events." *Washington Post*, August 12, 2007. Available online. URL: http://www.washingtonpost.com/wp-dyn/content/article/2007/08/08/AR2007080802038.html. Accessed on November 2, 2008.

17. Mendell, *Obama: From Promise to Power*, p. 147.

18. Obama, *The Audacity of Hope*, p. 132.

SENATOR OBAMA (PAGES 70–81)

1. Obama, *The Audacity of Hope*, p. 8.
2. *Ibid.*, p. 9.
3. *Ibid.*, p. 11.
4. *Ibid.*, p. 144.
5. David Mendell, "Ryan, Obama Enter New Ring; Democrat Carries High Hopes of Blacks with Him to Center Stage." *Chicago Tribune*, March 18, 2004, p. 1.
6. Monica Davey, "As Quickly as Overnight, a Democratic Star Is Born." *New York Times*, March 18, 2004, p. A20.
7. Bernstein, "The Speech."
8. Mendell, *Obama: From Promise to Power*, p. 271.
9. Pearson and Mendell, "Democrats: We've Got a Winner in Obama."
10. Obama, *The Audacity of Hope*, p. 250.
11. Pete Souza, *The Rise of Barack Obama* (Chicago: Triumph Books, 2008), p. 8.
12. *Ibid.*, p. 410
13. Mendell, *Obama: From Promise to Power*, pp. 308-309.
14. *Ibid.*, pp. 305, 312.
15. Garrett M. Graff, "The Legend of Barack Obama." *Washingtonian Magazine*, November 2006. Available online. URL: http://www.washingtonian.com/articles/mediapolitics/1836.html. Accessed on November 2, 2008.
16. "Resolution 1433, Lawfulness of Detentions by the United States in Guantánamo Bay." Parliamentary Assembly, Council of Europe, April 26, 2005. Available online: URL: http://assembly.coe.int/Main.asp?link=http://assembly.coe.int/Documents/AdoptedText/ta05/ERES1433.htm. Accessed on December 8, 2008.
17. *Ibid.*

HEADLINES FROM OBAMA'S TIME AS A PRESIDENTIAL CANDIDATE (PAGES 82–83)

1. Mark Knoller, "The Invisible Man of Campaign '08." CBS News, October 21, 2008. Available online. URL: http://www.cbsnews.com/stories/2008/10/21/politics/main4537119.shtml. Accessed on December 10, 2008.

MAKING HISTORY (PAGES 84–95)

1. Ted McClelland, "The Obama Juice." *Chicago Reader*, June 4, 2004. Available Online. URL: http://www.chicagoreader.com/obama/040604/. Accessed on December 8, 2008.
2. "Illinois Senator Barack Obama's Announcement Speech." *Washington Post*, February 10, 2007. Available online. URL: http://www.washingtonpost.com/wp-dyn/content/article/2007/02/10/AR2007021000879.html. Accessed on December 10, 2008.
3. *Ibid.*

4. Evan Thomas, "How He Did It." *Newsweek*, November 17, 2008. Available online. URL: http://www.newsweek.com/id/167582, Accessed on November 6, 2008.

5. David Broder, "Obama Finds His Address." *Washington Post*, December 23, 2007. Available online. URL: http://www.washingtonpost.com/wp-dyn/content/article/2007/12/21/AR2007122101923.html. Accessed on December 10, 2008.

6. Thomas, "How He Did It."

7. Ben Wallace-Wells, "Destiny's Child." *Rolling Stone*, February 22, 2007. Available online. URL: http://www.rollingstone.com/politics/story/13390609/campaign_08_the_radical_roots_of_barack_obama/print. Accessed on December 10, 2008.

8. "Complete Transcript of the *Sun-Times* Interview with Barack Obama." *Chicago Sun-Times*, March 15, 2008. Available online. URL: http://www.suntimes.com/news/politics/obama/844597,transcript031508.article. Accessed on December 1. 2008.

9. "Transcript of Obama's Speech." CNN, March 18, 2008. Available online. URL: http://www.cnn.com/2008/POLITICS/03/18/obama.transcript/index.html. Accessed on January 14, 2009.

10. Sandra Sobieraj Westfall, "The Obamas Get Personal." *People*, August 4, 2008. Available online. URL: http://www.people.com/people/archive/article/0,,20221617,00.html. Accessed on December 2, 2008.

11. Jann S. Wenner. "A Conversation with Barack Obama." *Rolling Stone*, July 10, 2008. Available online. URL: http://www.rollingstone.com/news/coverstory/21472234. Accessed on December 4, 2008.

12. Barack Obama, "The American Promise." August 28, 2008. Available online. URL: http://www.barackobama.com/2008/08/28/remarks_of_senator_barack_obam_108.php. Accessed on December 11, 2008.

13. Evan Thomas, "The Final Days." *Newsweek*, November 17, 2008. Available online. URL: http://www.newsweek.com/id/168017. Accessed on December 11. 2008.

14. Barack Obama, "Election Night Speech in Grant Park." November 4, 2008. Available online. URL: http://my.barackobama.com/page/community/post/stateupdates/gGx3Kc. Accessed on December 11. 2008.

15. David von Drehle, "Why History Can't Wait." *Time*, December 17, 2008. Available online. URL: http://www.time.com/time/specials/packages/printout/0,29239,1861543_1865068_1867013,00.html#. Accessed on January 13, 2009.

16. "Barack Obama's Inaugural Address." *New York Times*, January 20, 2009. Available online. URL: http://www.nytimes.com/2009/01/20/us/politics/20text-obama.html. Accessed on January 21, 2009.

17. *Ibid*.

18. "Remarks by the President on a New Beginning", 4 June 2009, http://www.whitehouse.gov/the_press_office/Remarks-by-the-President-at-Cairo-University-6-04-09/. Accessed on December 22, 2009.

19. "The Nobel Peace Prize for 2009, 9 October 2009, http://nobelprize.org/nobel_prizes/peace/laureates/2009/press.html. Accessed on December 22, 2009.

Further Reading

Abram, Carolyn, and Leah Pearlman. *Facebook for Dummies*. Hoboken, NJ: Wiley, 2008.

Bader, Bonnie. *Who Was Martin Luther King, Jr.?* New York: Grossett & Dunlap, 2008.

Bozonelis, Helen Koutras. *200 Years with Abraham Lincoln: One Man's Life and Legacy*. Berkeley Heights, NJ: Enslow Publishers, 2008.

Burgan, Michael. *Afghanistan*. Vero Beach, FL: Rourke Publishing, 2009.

Burgan, Michael. *Hillary Clinton: First Lady and Senator*. Minneapolis: Compass Point Books, 2008.

Cantwell, Rebecca. *Teens in Kenya*. Minneapolis: Compass Point Books, 2007.

Friedman, Lauri S. *The Iraq War*. Detroit: Greenhaven Press, 2008.

Gaines, Ann. *Hawaii*. New York: Benchmark Books, 2007.

Gormley, Beatrice. *Malcolm X: A Revolutionary Voice*. New York: Sterling Publishing, 2008.

Greene, Meg. *The Hunt for Osama bin Laden*. New York: Rosen Publishing Group, 2005.

Haley, Alex. *Roots*. Garden City, NY: Doubleday, 1976.

Halpern, Monica. *Moving North: African Americans and the Great Migration, 1915-1930*. Washington, D.C.: National Geographic, 2006.

Hurd, Owen. *Chicago History for Kids*. Chicago: Chicago Review Press, 2007.

Keller, Bill. *Tree Shaker: The Story of Nelson Mandela*. Boston: Kingfisher, 2008.

McClaurin, Irma. *The Civil Rights Movement*. Tarrytown, NY: Marshall Cavendish Benchmark, 2008.

Morgan, Sally. *Focus on Indonesia*. Stamford, CT: World Almanac Library, 2008.

Obama, Barack. *Dreams from My Father*. New York: Three Rivers Press, 2004.

Parks, Peggy J. *The Internet*. Detroit: Lucent Books, 2006.

Shields, Charles J. *Spike Lee*. Philadelphia: Chelsea House, 2002.

Taylor-Butler, Christine. *The Congress of the United States*. New York: Children's Press, 2008.

Thimmesh, Catherine. *Team Moon: How 400,000 People Landed Apollo 11 on the Moon*. Boston: Houghton Mifflin Company, 2006.

Thomas, Garen. *Yes We Can: A Biography of Barack Obama*. New York: Feiwel & Friends, 2008.

Wagner, Heather Lehr. *The Presidency*. New York: Chelsea House, 2007.

Find Out More

Abraham Lincoln
http://millercenter.org/academic/americanpresident/lincoln
> *This site from the University of Virginia has information on the life of the 16th U.S. president and the people who served in his cabinet, the group of his top advisors.*

Afghanistan's Future
http://news.bbc.co.uk/2/hi/in_depth/south_asia/2004/afghanistan/default.stm
> *The BBC provides detailed information about life in Afghanistan today and the ongoing challenges the Americans, British, and their allies face in creating a democratic government there.*

Barack Obama
http://www.chicagotribune.com/news/politics/obama/
> *One of Obama's hometown papers, the* Chicago Tribune, *offers the latest news and analysis on the president's actions.*

Barack Obama and Joe Biden
http://www.barackobama.com/index.php
> *The official site of the president and vice president, featuring a blog and links to Obama's pages on various social networking sites.*

Black History
http://www.gale.cengage.com/free_resources/bhm/
> *This site focuses on Black History Month, celebrated each February in the United States. It features biographies of famous African Americans and links to sites with more information.*

Cold War
http://www.cnn.com/SPECIALS/cold.war/
> *The Cable News Network maintains this site, which was created to go along with a 24-episode TV series on the Cold War. The site has complete transcripts of the episodes plus extra interviews and feature stories.*

The Democratic Party
http://www.democrats.org/page/content/victorytshirt/
> *The official website of the U.S. Democratic Party, with the latest party news and a review of general news headlines.*

Encyclopedia of Chicago
http://www.encyclopedia.chicagohistory.org/
> *A joint product of a history museum, a university, and a library, this online encyclopedia offers detailed information on the history of Obama's home city.*

HIV and AIDS in Africa
http://www.avert.org/aidsinafrica.htm
> *Avert, an international AIDS charity, provides a general history of the spread of AIDS and the battle to treat it. The group also has specific information on AIDS in different African nations.*

Iowa Caucus 2008
http://www.iowacaucus.org/iacaucus.html

This website explains the workings of the Iowa caucus, the first one held during every presidential campaign. Caucuses in other states are similar, though the exact rules may vary. Unlike a primary, caucuses let voters meet in small groups and talk about their favorite candidate before they vote for the delegates who represent each candidate.

Iraq War Debate 2002/2007
http://www.lib.umich.edu/govdocs/iraqwar.html

This site from the University of Michigan has a detailed list of links on all facets of the Iraq war from 2002 to 2007. The documents include news articles and government reports.

Presidents of the United States
http://www.potus.com/

This site has brief biographies on every U.S. president and provides links to more detailed online biographies.

The Republican Party
http://www.rnc.org/

The official U.S. Republican Party site has a history of the party as well as its position on important issues.

Roots
http://www.museum.tv/archives/etv/R/htmlR/roots/roots.htm

The Museum of Broadcast Communication discusses the content and the impact of this historic TV miniseries.

Save Darfur
http://www.savedarfur.org/content?splash=yes

A group of international charities and other organizations has created this site to provide information on the crisis in Darfur and seek help to end it.

Terrorism Research
http://www.terrorism-research.com/

This site has general information about terrorism, including its history, different types of terrorism, and the goals of terrorists. It provides links to sites that address how to fight terrorism and the specific efforts of the U.S. Department of Homeland Security.

Vietnam Online (Vietnam War)
http://www.pbs.org/wgbh/amex/vietnam/index.html

Based on a series developed for U.S. public television, this website traces the history of America's longest war. It includes copies of government documents and essays from people who were involved in the war.

Voices of Civil Rights
http://www.voicesofcivilrights.org/

A site with the history of the U.S. civil rights movement and the words of some of the people who worked for those rights.

The White House
http://www.whitehouse.gov/

The official website of the sitting U.S. president. Through at least January 2013, the site will have daily information on President Obama's actions and explain his policies.

Index